PROJECT
Relationship

THE ENTREPRENEUR'S
ACTION PLAN FOR PASSIONATE,
SUSTAINABLE LOVE

JOLI HAMILTON, PHD

Publishing Services provided by Paper Raven Books
Printed in the United States of America
First Printing, 2020

Paperback ISBN= 978-1-7353403-0-2
Hardback ISBN= 978-1-7353403-1-9

———————————❤———————————

For Ken, who made it fun to relearn how to love and who always remembers which spoon I like best.

———————————❤———————————

Table Of Contents

Preface

Take What Works, Leave the Rest

Hi, I'm Joli. My pronouns are she/her/hers. Sexuality, relationships, gender identity, and sexual orientation are complex personal experiences. I have used the pronouns she/her to describe my reader most of the time, and I often use he/him to describe their partners. Sometimes I use the singular "they" in my narratives because it more accurately reflects the clients whose stories I am sharing. I'll put this as plainly as I know how: Trans women are women. I am writing for women. To my readers who are nonbinary, gender fluid, gender queer, or who flip gender expectations: I value your experiences and affirm your reality. If this book happens to resonate with you, yay, welcome! To any men who find their way to these pages, welcome, and please note that I am intentionally centering on women's experiences. To my readers who practice ethical non-monogamy: Though you may have more than one partner, each dyad within your particular configuration contains the dynamic of the couple as well as the multivalent whole. I have found that these ideas apply no matter how many partners are involved.

I have spent thousands of hours (and many thousands of dollars too!) learning how to make sense of relationships. I crash and burned one marriage and began another with a lot of hope and even more fear— fear I would repeat old patterns and make the same mistakes, fear that I was just not cut out to be happily in love. As I finished my doctorate in depth psychology, I was inspired to take the knowledge I had worked so hard for and create an action-centered guide for women like me who want <u>more</u> from every aspect of their life, including big, passionate love. We don't have to choose between our dream careers and the love we long for. In fact, it begins with the very same kind of focus that you use to make your business sizzle.

The last 11 years have been a time of intense learning for me—both in the rollercoaster of family life and in academic study. The academics path I chose left me with some particular language. Though I'm not a fan of jargon, I love having added some of the words of depth psychology to my life because they describe things I just didn't have words for before. You'll see me use the word "soul," for instance, and I don't mean soul in the sense of any particular religion. Soul for me means the subjective experience of being you, the unrepeatable spark of wonder that you are in the universe. There are other words like "psyche" and "complexes" that I'll explain along the way. Some of them are probably ideas you are familiar with, while some might be new. You might use a different word to describe those ideas—that's cool with me. I use whatever ideas get results. I don't care what we call them. What matters is that they work to create more loving relationships.

I am excited to enter into a discussion about love and business with you. I'm certain I will have made mistakes, and I welcome your feedback. I will keep striving to do better. I understand that my experience is limited by my white privilege. I acknowledge that I am writing this book on land forcibly taken from the Pocumtuc and Mahican peoples and that the violence of my ancestors has not been appropriately redressed. Anti-racist work and reparative actions are not someone else's problem. It is my work to do, and I commit to doing it every day.

Before We Begin

This book is meant to provide you with practical ideas you can put to use today. It is meant to be a jumping-off point for you to create the habits and rituals of love that will work best for your unique relationship and business situation. I believe everyone has the opportunity to live their love each day. That said, I also know that sometimes we find ourselves in a life we didn't expect.

We don't control everything that happens to us, and no amount of positivity or "intent to manifest" will overcome systemic oppression or abusive behavior. If you are struggling because you are disabled, unable to access medical care, live in poverty (people in business, working their butts off, can still be poor), experience racial injustice, sexual or gender discrimination, or any other systemic abuse, I want to say that I see you. I understand that some of the suggestions that would work for someone not facing those issues won't be a good fit for your life. I don't have all the answers, and I haven't faced what you face. I hope you find pieces of this book that do help, but it is even more critical that you trust yourself to know if a particular exercise or suggestion is not suitable for you.

If you are reading this book and thinking about how your partner isn't open to problem-solving, isn't listening to your pain, or worse, is thinking about how they would injure, threaten, or coerce you, these are signs that your relationship is in need of more intensive help than any book can provide. I urge you to seek professional help as soon as you possibly can. This book is not intended to replace the advice of a trusted counselor or to convert an abusive partner into a loving one—that work needs a personal interface.

Project Relationship: Master Checklist

Chapter 2 Empowered Relating
- ☐ Tool: Somatic Awareness
- ☐ Assessment: Who Are You Today?
- ☐ Assessment: Entrepreneurial Strengths
- ☐ Action Step: The Struggle

Chapter 3 Boundaries, the Invitation to Intimacy
- ☐ Assessment: How Do You Handle Challenging Boundaries?
- ☐ Action Step: Recognize Your Yes

Chapter 4 Who Is This Person?
- ☐ Assessment: Recognizing Individuality
- ☐ Assessment: Love Languages

Chapter 5 Relationship Resilience
- ☐ Tool: Building Ritual Template
- ☐ Action Step: Building Ritual
- ☐ Assessment: My Relationship "Why"
- ☐ Assessment: Noticing Your Sore Spots
- ☐ Assessment: What Really Matters?
- ☐ Action Step: Who's Responsible?

Chapter 6 Courageous Connecting
- ☐ Assessment: Unmasking Your True Self
- ☐ Action Step: The Curiosity Date

Chapter 1

Getting By, Wanting More

I was standing in the driveway, balancing four cartons of eggs from the chickens in my backyard and trying to convince all seven kids they needed to get in the car <u>now</u> so I could beat my first clients to the gym for the 6 AM class. It turns out there is only so much chill I can manage. When my partner popped out of the house, oblivious to my mood, striding towards the car to join us and said, "Do the kids all have their water bottles?" I lost it. I lost my chill, I lost my temper, and messiest of all, I lost the eggs…all over my own shoes.

The word "entrepreneur" comes from the French *entreprendre*, which is a verb that translates to undertake, to manage, to <u>do</u> something. That morning, the last word I would have used to describe myself was entrepreneur. I didn't feel like someone who was managing, but I was definitely doing something. A million somethings, it seemed. Every second something or someone needed my attention: the gym I was running, the kids, the house, the classes I was taking, then of course there was my partner and the relationship we promised each other. There was a never-ending stream of doing, doing, doing.

This big energy and insatiable ambition to do, do, do was part of the sparkle that initially attracted my husband. But as I stood in the driveway covered in eggs and expletives, all that <u>doing</u> was definitely not a good look. I had uncorked the overwhelm of it all and the passion that spewed forth was not the kind anyone wants to receive at 5:30 AM. Since my clients needed my attention right away and my kids needed their mom to pull herself together, I cut from the one place that seemed negotiable: my marriage.

Yeah, that worked exactly as well as you're imagining. Things got...rocky...to say the least. I started leaning into my least effective relationship habits. I hoped he would read my mind (though I would never admit it at the time). I expected him to hold up his family responsibilities (but stopped spending time collaborating on setting our family priorities). I went to bed thinking about marketing strategies and how to convince my middle schooler that algebra wasn't going to kill her (but I didn't remember that lying next to me was the love of my life). This was the person who inspired me to toss my life into the wood-chipper only a few short years ago. He was fascinating, kind, and beautiful. And I had no time to worry about any of that.

It was bleak. I thought about leaving and wondered if I just didn't have what it takes to do marriage—sticking it out through a disconnected, overwhelming few decades only to look at each other when the kids are grown and say: Who the heck are you?

I considered leaving many, many times.

The turning point for me happened in one moment. I was lying next to this guy, who had been pissing me off and letting me down for months, and all at once I realized that I had never actually <u>decided</u> to make this work. Really work for both of us. When I ran into a problem in any one of the dozen businesses I had started, I didn't give up and I certainly didn't wait for the problem to solve itself. I made a choice and changed the only thing I could: me. Every time I decided to solve the problems, I found a way. This was no different.

I turned to him in bed and told him my deepest desire: I wanted the passion and fire that we had started with and I wanted to feel safe and secure. I was shaking and had the covers pulled over my eyes. It felt like jumping off a building because I was admitting that 1) I wasn't happy and 2) I needed more. It felt like he might say no. I told him I wanted to start over and make the relationship that we had dreamed of on those first few hormone-laden dates. That morning was the beginning of our eyes-wide-open-show-up-do-the-hard-stuff new life.

Your moment of clarity might have already happened or maybe this is it, right now, reading this story. You don't have to settle for a boring home any more than you have to settle for a boring job. You already have what it takes; you just need to learn how to apply your natural entrepreneurial spirit to your love life too.

Running a business built from nothing isn't for everyone. It's not just that it takes a ton of energy to build, grow, and run your business. Sure, it does take energy but not just any old kind. Being an entrepreneur means you bring inspiration, initiative, dedication, and decisiveness every day. You look at the big picture and manage details. To be a bit cliché, you contain multitudes, and it shows. In fact, plenty of studies have shown that entrepreneurs score high on qualities like persistence, initiative, vision, and resilience. Lucky for us, these exact qualities are also the difference between a boring, frustrating marriage and one that gives us rock-solid stability and deep passionate fun. You've already got the keys; you just need to learn how to apply them in love as well as you do in business.

If entrepreneurs have all this potential for kick-ass relationships, then why the hell are so many of us spending years just barely scraping by in marriages that drain our souls? I believe it is mostly because we forget to bring our whole selves into our love life. We start a relationship with all the best intentions, but then we fall into habits of relating that are less than optimal and sometimes downright destructive. We settle for less than we want, and we guard against having to give too much. I've been there. After years of just getting by but never really being happy, I ended my first marriage abruptly. Once it was over, I didn't know what I wanted from a relationship going forward but I knew I couldn't be satisfied by anything less than the full catastrophe of deep intimacy. But the day-to-day grind of life made me tuck that idea away. "There's time for love and romance later," I told myself. "Build something of your own now."

I don't regret building that business. It was fun and hard, and it helped me develop confidence I never knew I had. But I do wish I hadn't chopped my life up into little compartments. I didn't actually have to choose between a purposeful career and a passionate marriage. I needed to apply my persistence, risk tolerance, intuition, and drive to my whole life, including my love life. Entrepreneurs know how to give their all and what I've seen is that they can do that at home and in business at the same time. In fact, the more comfortable they are at using their entrepreneurial skills at home, the more satisfied they are with all aspects of their life. And, as a bonus, relationship satisfaction is a big win for your business too!

Chapter 2

Empowered Relating

You are not helpless in your relationship, but you might be living <u>as if</u> you are helpless and that causes trouble. I have good news for you: Relationships are systems. Systems respond to change, especially change from within. Do you know how you respond to changes in your market? For example, when a competitor beats your value proposition or your website gets completely wiped by accident, you don't just sigh and hope things change. You take stock of the situation, of your strengths and weaknesses, and <u>you make changes</u> to respond to the new developments. You affect the system yourself by responding thoughtfully to it. It's time to take that same attitude into your loving relationships. It's go time.

Good News

Your relationship will respond to your changes because it is not an autonomous creature. If your marriage is falling apart, it's the people in the marriage who have opportunities to learn and grow. It's pretty common to hear people talk about their relationship as if it has rights and responsibilities, joys and sorrows—in other words, to imagine it as a person. I'm a depth psychologist; we LOVE to personify things, which means to use our imagination to breathe life into inanimate or abstract ideas. Personification can be a valuable psychological move. Personifying abstract ideas like love, death, or money helps me to feel the complexity of things I can't quite put my finger on.

When it comes to our relationship though, many of us take this to a dangerous extreme. We forfeit our ability to create the relationship we want when we imagine our relationship as a thing happening to us. When we are in that mindset, we say things about how our partner just won't change. We have passive-aggressive battles that put more and more distance between us and the partner we say we love. But your marriage isn't a separate thing acting upon you and your partner. It's not happening to you, it is you, and that is good news.

Knowing this puts your relationship happiness back where it belongs: in your hands.

Throughout this book, I will be asking you to take action. There are plenty of books that theorize about love and do it well. Those books inform my approach to mentoring you in developing relationship skills. But theory without action will get you nowhere. I recommend writing down your thoughts as we go along. Grab a journal or even write in the margins, but take the action each step of the way. This is it. TAKE ACTION. You are empowered to make changes in your relationships; no one else can give you that power. Just start with yourself.

Many of the ideas in this book will be even more powerful if your partner wants to do them too. For instance, if you want to make a change in your sex life, it's pretty awesome to talk with the person you want to have sex <u>with</u>. Make these parts fun. I've intentionally designed these partnered action steps to take 90 minutes or less. Many are only 10 to 30 minutes of shared time! You could do all of the assessments and action steps together, if your partner wants to, but it's not required. Don't guilt anyone into it—that will only make tension. Focus on <u>your</u> participation and commit yourself to the adventure of living lovingly. Change is possible. A passionate, peaceful, and purposeful relationship is within reach.

Tool: Somatic Awareness

This is a short exercise, but it is a critical skill to add to your toolbox as you start this project of actively creating your dream relationship. You can do this anywhere; no need to close your eyes or take on a meditative posture. Just be where you are, as you are now.

Right now, wherever you are, shift your attention from reading this book to being in your body.

Feel the edges of your "you."

Do you feel spread out thin or tightly compacted? Is your body feeling airy, soft, stiff, open, saggy? Are you aware of any numbness, buzzing, or floatiness? Do you feel any sensations that are hard to name?

It is tempting to answer with "I feel tired," but right now move deeper and get more specific than tired. (I know you are tired—you run a business and keep your home life going!) Do your best to give each sensation a name even if you aren't sure you have the right word. You can write those words down or hold them in your mind for a few moments.

Now, take three deep breaths.

Your body has a wisdom of its own. Often the body and the conscious mind, that part of you that is reading and thinking about this book, aren't in alignment. That is alright. This is an opportunity to be aware of how complex your experience is. You can feel more than one thing at a time. You are magnificently human! Noticing how your body feels as well as how many different emotions and thoughts are bubbling around all at once is a foundational skill for creating a loving relationship.

Noticing is all that is necessary for now.

Self-Awareness, the Master Skill for Relationships

I could have written this book for just anyone, I suppose. Most people want to be in relationships and most of us struggle to be happy once we are in them. The information I share could be taken up by almost anyone. But I didn't write this book for just anyone. I wrote it for you, the woman entrepreneur, because you are spectacularly well equipped to exchange mediocre relationships for deep, joyful love.

It's no accident you are an entrepreneur. The qualities that make you effective in business are deeply embedded in you. One recent study found that entrepreneurs tend to be more proactive, independent, and able to tolerate risk. And a Gallup survey determined the top 10 qualities of successful entrepreneurial types included an ability to develop relationships and confidently follow their own path. Most importantly, according to this study, the entrepreneur who has an ability to be honest with themselves also has the most potential to build something astonishing. I agree completely that this is the crucial factor in your ability to transform your life. Honest reflection translates into deep self-awareness. A self-aware person can lean on their strengths and learn to manage their weak spots with grace.

One of the biggest lies I hear my clients tell me is that relationships are supposed to be simple. If the relationship isn't simple, they can quickly give me a list of what their partner is doing that is making everything so complicated and miserable. They disown the power they actually have by assigning blame rather than looking at the complex system their relationship is and recognizing their place in that system.

If your best friend came to you saying the only way for her business to perform better is if her <u>customers</u> change, you would set her straight, right? You'd remind her that the only things she can control in this world are her own thoughts, feelings, and actions, so if she wants change, she'd better look in the mirror and stop shifting the blame onto her customers.

It's not that all of our partners are perfect just the way they are. They have crappy habits and unhelpful patterns. Their baggage comes up and gets messy. With a bit of luck and communication, maybe they will decide to work on some of that stuff. But if you don't start doing your work and looking directly at your part of the puzzle, then you will never see anything change. You don't have a responsibility to change your partner. Period. You have a responsibility to take charge of your life.

I've been there, hoping that if my partner would just change what he was doing, we could finally be happy. It was a toxic sludge that poisoned whatever chance we might have had together.

I didn't have the easiest childhood, but there was always food on the table, and I knew where my parents were all the time. They didn't seem to "get" me, but they also didn't want me to be miserable. With that said, home never really felt stable. My mom, despite her deep love for us, struggled with wild swings in her mood. When she'd walk through the door after work, you never knew if you'd be met with rage, tears, or a smile. My dad didn't seem to understand how hard this made my life. My little brother was a sensitive little guy willing to do anything to avoid the rages. I learned from a young age to be bold and take responsibility for everyone else's feelings. I tried to shift the energy from anger or sadness, and I stepped up to do a lot more adulting than was reasonable for a child.

This is what I showed up with in my first marriage. My husband had his own history to work out; he wasn't without scars. But my mistake was hoping I would feel safer, happier, and more loved if I took responsibility for his feelings and actions the way I tried to do in my childhood home.

Our marriage didn't fall apart immediately. We made quite a life together, in fact. There were business ventures to start and children to raise, friends to share our time with and family to count on. But I was rarely satisfied. I felt unseen and unheard most of the time. I wanted him to change the way he related to me. He wanted the same, sending me off to therapy twice to deal with my issues. We stayed locked into our protective stances—warriors pitted against each other without even realizing it. I tended to get needy and fill with rage, while he would go silent and withdraw completely.

And so it went, each of us with all-too-easy ways to shift the responsibility for change away from ourselves.

Then, fairly suddenly, I didn't want to live like that anymore. I didn't understand how not to keep enacting my old habits though, and before long that meant I was done with my marriage.

I'm not here to tell you whether you are better off in your relationship or moving on. I'm here to tell you that until I decided to become profoundly responsible for my own fears and anger, there was no point in worrying about what my ex was doing with his. Self-awareness is the silver bullet that can lead to a life in alignment with your soul. It hasn't been easy to reclaim all of the parts of myself I had disowned and to build new patterns, but it worked. Life is still full of challenges, but now I can center love without constantly reenacting the habits of disconnection I learned as a child. I can love with more of myself available to my kids and my partner. I can love myself enough to own even the ugly bits of my past.

Assessment: Who Are You Today?

Before you proceed with these questions, take a deep breath and exhale fully. Notice where you are feeling tightness. Breathe again and open up what space you can. There is no need to change anything. Just be present as you are now.

- Three words that describe your business today:

- Three words that describe how you are showing up in your business right now:

- Three words that describe your relationship today:

- Three words that describe how you show up in the relationship:

- Three words that describe how your partner shows up (from your view) in the relationship:

The way you are feeling about your life today is just that: the way you feel <u>today</u>. It isn't a measure of your goodness or worth. It's just where you are. So if things feel a little bleak or dark, don't worry. If they feel awesome but unreliable, that's okay. You picked up this book looking for a shift, and knowing where you are now is the only way to actually know if you are successfully changing your life. You are holding a roadmap to a more satisfying and stable life in your hands. This is just the beginning.

Owning Your Strengths

To develop our self-awareness muscles, let's start by looking at our strengths. You aren't just one thing; you are a multivalent wonder. Even on the toughest days, you are enough just as you are. Are you in the habit of claiming your strengths or of denying your awesomeness? Most of us are simultaneously accomplishing amazing things and beating ourselves up for not being enough. Recognizing the strength in yourself matters. You can work on your weaknesses every day, making incremental improvements, but if you constantly deny your strengths, demurring from people's compliments, refusing to acknowledge all that you are, turning weaknesses into strengths won't matter much, will it? For a whole bunch of social reasons, it is tempting to focus on complimenting others and tearing ourselves down. I know that you are enough just as you are. I've spent the past 15 years working with women as a doula, athletic trainer, and psychological coach. Every. Single. One. of them has been an amazing collection of strengths, whether they knew it or not. But once they recognized those qualities, they were unstoppable.

Time to get real. Today, you are going to honor the immense effort you have undertaken to become you. The challenges of growing up, of learning how the world works through experience and education, of starting your first business—of living your life story—deserve to be valued. Humans are interesting critters. We use labels so that we can share our reality with others, but lots of folks say they don't like labels. Often what we mean when we push back against labels is that we don't want to wear the labels other people have placed on us. Have you ever been called something that just felt wrong? I have, and that label took more than a decade to shake off!

Assessment: Entrepreneurial Strengths

This exercise is about claiming the labels that work for you. Naming your strengths and claiming them is a part of owning your past and designing your future.

Step 1. Set a timer for two minutes.

Step 2. Circle every word that resonates with you. Aim for 20 or more. Don't worry about needing to be "the best" before you circle an item. Trust your intuition and circle words that you feel represent parts of you, even if those parts are tough for you to claim.

Courage	Kindness	Clever
Risk Tolerance	Rigorous	Prudence
Optimism	Energetic	Practical
Initiative	Fairness	Content
Orderly	Adventurous	Belonging
Imaginative	Spontaneity	Calm
Leadership	Selflessness	Freedom
Innovation	Security	Cautious
Persistence	Wellness	Gentle
Sensitive	Grace	Self-actualizing
Inspiration	Speed	Professional
Resourcefulness	Inquisitive	Ingenious
Generosity	Peaceful	Dynamic
Assertiveness	Growth-oriented	Decisive
Flexibility	Consistent	Courtesy
Focus	Helpful	Creative
Balance	Control	Serene
Cheerfulness	Fidelity	Measured

Simplicity	Orderly	Honest
Structured	Family-oriented	Positive
Honorable	Wild	Prepared
Strategic	Punctual	Supportive
Quick	Shrewd	Harmonious
Restrained	Clear-minded	Insightful
Expressive	Competitive	Clear
Traditional	Service-oriented	Joyful
Strong	Dedicated	Pious
Bold	Virtuosity	Spontaneous
Team-oriented	Ambitious	Just
Accepting	Cooperative	Grateful
Visionary	Curious	Understanding
Altruistic	Enthusiastic	Unique
Individuating	Wise	Empathetic
Pragmatic	Clear	Active

Step 3. Set a new timer for two minutes.

Step 4. Look at the items you circled and find five that you could claim easily.

Step 5. Looking at your five words, how did you get those strengths? Do they feel like they were always with you, just something you were born with? Did you develop them in response to difficulties? Did you have a mentor or role model who guided you to develop these qualities?

You are immeasurably more than this list. Each of these strengths is only one tiny facet of your multiplicity.

For now, it is enough to simply recognize and claim them. You are on an adventure of creating more love, starting with loving the wonder that is you.

Welcoming Struggle

At least as important as knowing your strengths is knowing where you consistently struggle. A while back, I started teaching my kids that struggling is really learning and we noticed a big transformation in our household relationship to struggle. What do I mean by struggle? I mean the feeling that you get when you have an idea in mind but your attempts to actualize the idea just keep falling short. You hear the perfection of a new song in your head, but you sit at the piano and the notes keep feeling choppy and harsh. You imagine a thick, chewy, warm chocolate chip cookie but you open the oven to find most of yours are lopsided and a bit thin. You dream up a fresh new idea for inspiring women to transform their lives and relationships, but the first draft of your book has big gaps in it. (Guess who that one happened to?)

If we give up on struggling, the clunky idea never gets a chance to be refined. We never get the chance to see our ideas inspire others. Our art never sees the light of day.

Change one thing and you can create so much more in your life: <u>Welcome the struggle.</u>

Struggle + Acceptance = Learning to dance
with the world <u>just the way it is</u>

It's not struggling that is the problem anyway. Struggling is the act of trying, falling short, adjusting, and trying again. We keep at it until we find the groove and our idea finally takes the form we envisioned. Struggling is just what it feels like to be in your personal growth zone. But, ugh, can it feel icky if we are in love with the idea that everything should be fluid and come easily to us.

Let's be clear, I don't mean we should flail around wildly, just taking action without thought or assessment. I mean the belief that what you are doing should be easy, and if it's not then it's not your thing—that belief can go sit down.

Rather than pick something easy, give yourself the space to approach your struggles with ease. Let yourself play out at the edge of what's comfortable, making things that are less than perfect.

Maybe you do this <u>really</u> well when it comes to your work. Your business benefits from your ability to envision something grand, design your offering, create solutions for your ideal customer. You try those out, evaluate how well they work, adjust your processes to make everything work better and repeat, repeat, repeat. This is the basic flow of what I call easeful struggle. I find it fairly straightforward when it comes to business ideas. Hey, no one said it would be easy to make something awesome on the first try, right? But when it comes to our relationships, for some reason we throw this all out the window. Sure, there's the old adage "marriage takes work." But what is that work, exactly? What does it mean to work on my relationships?

The work I'm talking about is a constant struggle. Wait, that sounds bad. The work I'm talking about is a constant easeful determination to learn about myself and my partner as we live our lives. That sounds better. It's the same message with a different attitude behind it.

The struggle of being with someone, allowing yourself to be seen, and noticing your faults in the mirror of the Other is not easy. It also doesn't end. We will always be learning in relationships. You won't get to skip the struggle if you want to experience your relationship at its full potential. But if you approach it with easefulness, the struggle becomes your guide. Over time, you will feel yourself struggling and know that this is the process of learning and growing. You will lean into it and trust that what you feel today will transform. You are becoming.

The toughest part about learning is wishing it felt different. When my oldest child was about six years old, she was really impatient with our reading lessons. I was homeschooling her and we only worked on reading for 15 to 20 minutes each day, but she just wasn't having it. Finally, one day she said, "I want to go to school." I wasn't totally against this, but my extremely introverted, quiet little girl hated big groups and unfamiliar settings.

Needless to say, I was pretty surprised. I asked her why. "Because I want the teacher to teach me how to read. This is too hard." I wasn't sure I got it, so I asked her what she thought the teacher would do to teach her to read. Turns out she hoped that a teacher could save her from the pains of learning. Instead of phonics, this creative little girl hoped for a more magic-wand approach to reading. She's in college now, with excellent grades born entirely of her own determination and grit; it all worked out. But that moment is seared into my mind. Sage taught me one of the most valuable lessons of my life that day.

Trying to understand what she was going through, I started paying attention to what learning a new subject felt like for me. YUCK. It wasn't awesome. Learning didn't really feel good in my body, it was hard. Paying really close attention, I noticed all kinds of sensations in my body when I was struggling/learning.

On the upside, now that Sage had helped me locate this information, my ability to learn got quite a boost. The process went faster because I stopped fighting the discomfort of the struggle. I stopped blaming myself for not knowing already and just let myself do the work, trusting that eventually the struggle would ease. Eventually, I proved this point to myself by mastering math classes as an adult after failing them over and over again as a teen. I still get the same sensations, but now they aren't traumatizing. They are welcome signs that everything is chugging right along in my learning.

Action Step: The Struggle

Step 1. Think of something you need to learn right now that you can use to take note of the sensations of learning in your body. Maybe you need to learn how to manage spreadsheets or how to craft a new funnel for your latest offering or how to speak enough of a new language to go on vacation to your dream destination. If you can, pick something you've been avoiding.

Turn off distractions and put your phone in another room. Set a timer for 30 minutes to dive into it. Do the work. Be in the struggle. Learn and stretch.

Step 2. When the timer goes off, turn on the part of you that notices bodily sensations.

Are your ears hot? Are you biting your lip? Does everything feel fuzzy, tight, or watery? Does your butt want to move from the chair? Are your eyes closing? Is drowsiness taking over? Are you reaching for your phone?

Step 3. Describe the sensations in a couple of sentences.

Step 4. Bingo! You've discovered your learning/ struggle clues. Those sensations can be a cue rather than a distraction. While this takes some mindfulness, it is really effective at increasing your ability to get out of your own way and learn more easily.

Step 5. Now you are going to enlist some backup to make welcoming the struggle even easier. Your partner probably has an inkling when you are giving off the I'm-uncomfortably-stretching-and-growing vibe, but now is the time to <u>tell</u> your partner what you know about your struggle/learning cues. Somewhere along the line, we all got the idea that true love means never having to explain our secret inner thoughts and feelings; if it's real love they'll just know. Toss that whole idea in the garbage! You want to be understood and to understand them, so don't try to work without a map. <u>Tell them</u> you fiddle with your hair or bite your lip when you are trying to learn something new. Share with them what it feels like to be at your growing edge and ask them what it's like for them. Sharing this info invites your partner to know you a bit more and that is intimacy.

Step 6. Finally, make a sticky note with <u>your</u> specific learning sensation cues on it. Label the note "I'm learning" at the top and hang it where you are likely to be when you are struggling. Over your desk is one place, but I have a note just like this written in Sharpie on my home gym wall too. When I feel my personal struggle sensations, the note helps me to remember that this is when I am growing and changing. This feeling is not my enemy, it is my path forward. When your struggle signals come in, remind yourself that learning isn't always comfortable and that's okay. You can be in the learning sensations. You will stretch and grow.

Key Takeaways

Relationships are systems, which means you can create change by starting with yourself. You are empowered to begin making your relationship experience work for you.

- Take an inventory of your entrepreneurial strengths and notice how those strengths can be applied to your relationship.

- Welcome the sense of struggle as evidence that you have broken out of your rut and you are now learning new relationship skills.

- Learn to notice what your body sensations are when you are at your growing edge. Write them down and tell your partner about what struggling and learning look like for you.

Chapter 3

Boundaries, the Invitation to Intimacy

What exactly are boundaries? Boundaries are the lines between you and me. Where you end and I begin. Boundaries protect the soul, heart, and body from being overrun by an overwhelmingly complicated world. Boundaries are how we identify what is mine and what is yours. Boundaries aren't objective; they are created, by choice, by us. There is no universal set of boundaries because they have to do with our individuality. Boundaries are physical, mental, emotional, political, and more.

An example of a boundary commonly understood in the U.S. is personal space. It's that invisible bubble around your body that feels like it belongs to you. The personal space boundary you hold is likely different for a stranger and your lover. You might compromise your typical personal space boundary in order to catch the next elevator but absolutely draw the line on that level of closeness to strangers in most other situations. Boundaries are challenging for many people, in part due to this inherent flexibility. When we learn how to set strong, flexible, resilient boundaries, we can let others get really close to us and feel safe at the same time. In other words, boundary setting is a key skill for intimacy.

Boundaries mean little without a full understanding of the context in which they are drawn, which takes time and communication. Boundaries work best when everyone involved shares a willingness to pay attention to the context. You know that saying, "read the room"? It's code for take everything in, look around, pay attention. Not everyone is willing. Some people will intentionally manipulate the fluid nature of boundaries in order to get what they desire without appearing to breach any rules.

The recent uptick in conversations about consent brought on by the #MeToo movement's increased exposure resulted in quite a backlash from people who want two things: They want boundaries to be concrete (in other words, rules not subject to interpretation) and that they be able to pick and choose which ones they have to follow (in other words, just so long as they get to interpret all rules for themselves).

Two things I know to be true about boundaries: They are fluid and they require consistent communication. A flat, fixed boundary is an okay starting point, but over time many boundaries in our most intimate relationships will need to develop nuance. Just because someone else wants you to doesn't mean you'll sacrifice your boundaries or that your boundaries need to flex, ever. Absolutely not. But your boundaries, if strongly developed, can allow you to explore the world more fully. If you know your boundaries, you can communicate your hard "no" and your "hell yes" with conviction, making space for yourself in the world. Firm, clear boundaries are an asset to all relationships. Now, how do we get some?

What about Consent?

One of the hats I wear is sex educator. I work with teens, college students, and adults on a huge range of sexuality topics. Lately, I've been getting a lot of questions about teaching teens how consent works. Only very rarely do the adults asking think about how consent works in their own relationships. This is a missed opportunity. I'm grateful that the #MeToo movement has created some more consistent discussion about consent, but there is a very long way to go to achieve healthy relating as a standard in our culture.

The word "consent" gives many people the impression that it is a thing to be obtained, like a signature on a contract. This is completely off base. Consent is about boundaries in the fluid realm of relationship. In other words, consent in established relationships is an ongoing negotiation of needs and wants. This might sound worrisome. Some pretty loud people with pretty big microphones have been hollering about how this new idea of consent is impossible because it isn't fixed, solid, and unchangeable. But you are way smarter than that. You understand that relationships are always changing because people are growing, learning, feeling, and thinking. We don't need to offer each other notarized documents; we need to learn how to set and hold our boundaries and respect the ones our partners have. There is a magic that happens when we learn how to set boundaries that are fluid yet strong, and that rests on a foundation of self-respect. Once we learn that, we have a new capacity for intimacy. Bottom line: Boundary work can be tough for some folks, but it has phenomenal power to deepen intimacy between partners.

Boundaries Begin with Self-Awareness

I believe self-awareness is a master tool for a reason. Underneath all the millions of decisions you must make each year, behind all the dreams you have is... you. Without knowing yourself really well, you will inevitably drift along in life without following your calling or making your dreams happen. Self-awareness isn't always fun, but it is always an investment in you. Getting to know your edges lets you decide whether to go explore those edges and when to invite select others into your inner being. The benefits are huge. If you don't know your boundaries, there is a high chance that you are letting other folks determine how your day-to-day life goes. And as go the moments, so goes your life.

Almost everyone I meet has some trouble with boundary setting. We tend toward extremes without realizing it. Some people have overly soft boundaries and feel like they have to do whatever it takes to fulfill requests, even unspoken ones. Other people have rigid boundaries that keep them from feeling overrun by other people's needs and wants but also make it almost impossible to develop an intimate connection.

When I was younger, I had a reputation for being quite a hard-ass. Cross my lines and you would feel the repercussions. Okay, I think I still have that reputation, but I also have a lot more skill at delivering the news that my boundaries are crossed. Even better, I learned (the hard way) that communicating my boundaries through words and nonverbal signals can be done with kindness.

My early brashness was born out of necessity. Too often as a child I was asked to do things that were really grown-up jobs: take care of my parents' emotions, find ways to stop adult arguments, and do whatever it takes to keep my very sensitive brother from falling apart. The pressure to take care of other adults didn't let up even as I gained some independence and had my own children who needed my care. I was responsible for the finances of my parents and I handled the deaths of my grand-aunt and grandmother, including all the complicated estate work. This was all before I was 26. To be honest, it was all a little too much. I gained a ton of skills, but I became rigid in my boundary setting and hostile to anyone who asked me to do things for them, even when they were things I wanted to do.

In retrospect, I see that I had burned out by 27 years old. I had three kids under five and all those extended family responsibilities. In addition, my mother's chronic illness became much worse, requiring a liver transplant. She had been a wonderful and involved grandparent, but now she needed intense care too. I had an unmanaged chronic migraine problem and I was running multiple small business ventures—three of my own at the time, plus one my husband was just starting to cook up.

I had developed the habit of brash hostility to hold my boundaries. I guess it was better than no boundaries at all, but it didn't actually work very well. The hostility isolated me from many who might have been good friends. Some people saw through it, but I definitely didn't know how to moderate my desperation with kindness, even towards my friends.

When I blew up my world by leaving my first husband, many things changed. One that was not clear at the time was how I created and communicated my boundaries.

First, I went through what I now see as a total meltdown. I lost touch with my core so profoundly that I no longer recognized myself. I didn't know who I was. My therapist seemed to think I was safe, that I was in a chrysalis. You know, in that phase where the caterpillar turns to goo.

I don't know if I'd call myself a butterfly, but when I emerged, I had gained a different way of sharing myself with the world. My communication was clearer, and I learned (through a lot of trial and error) how to deliver it with love. My relationships changed. Some people from that time are distant memories, but others I have had the pleasure to come to know in a new way. We share our boundaries explicitly and respect each other deeply.

Michelle's struggle with boundaries looked very different than mine. She disliked confrontation and really hated the feeling that came when she set a firm limit. After weeks, months, or even years of accepting something, she would finally tell her partner, Chris. The last big fight at their house came when Michelle told Chris that she wasn't going to do the bookkeeping for their shared business anymore. Except, that's not how Chris found out. Instead, he came back from a meeting and found Michelle explaining their entire financial situation to a stranger at the kitchen table. Chris was confused and angry and didn't react well, to say the least.

It turns out Michelle had been dropping hints about wanting to not have to handle the bookkeeping for two years. Chris thought the comments were just her way of getting attention for doing a hard job, so he responded with cheerleading and motivation. This drove Michelle bonkers because she didn't want to feel more obligated. She wanted out. But Michelle never actually said no. As the months piled up, so did her resentment. When she finally hit her limit, she solved the issue of hating the bookkeeping, but she created a new problem between herself and Chris. Boundary setting isn't optional in a healthy interdependent relationship. Michelle needed to learn how to find and then communicate her boundaries. It wasn't easy, but it was the pivotal move for her. To be able to share her limits and desires, she first needed to learn how to recognize and set her boundaries.

Setting a boundary can feel harsh if you were trained to ignore your needs. You might feel like you won't be loved or like you'll be punished if you set your limits. It will take practice. Shaming yourself because you have overly rigid or overly soft boundaries won't help. This is a skill—something you will get better at with practice. It is not a measure of your worth.

Exploring boundaries in safe ways is an exceptionally great investment in your happiness. By focusing on what you feel—really listening to those inner voices and sensations—you will come to know yourself more intimately. These exercises are designed for you alone. Please don't skip this part. If you currently have a strong sense of your boundaries, this will be a time to check in; we change, sometimes without noticing. If you struggle with knowing your boundaries, this is an absolutely necessary first step. Before you can learn how to communicate your boundaries, you need to have a clear sense of what they are.

Later, in the chapter on intimacy, you will have the opportunity to explore boundaries with your partner and to develop new ways to communicate them to each other. For now, let this be all for you—a self-care skill of immense value. Start by exploring professional situations for boundary trouble.

Assessment: How Do You Handle Challenging Boundaries?

- Name a boundary that is difficult for you to hold in business:

- Do you have a hard time holding most boundaries or a select few?

- Do the boundaries you struggle with have a common theme or a particular context (i.e., money-related, family stuff, truth telling, vulnerability, scapegoating, responsibility, control, connection, safety, etc.)?

- What does it feel like for you to have your boundaries crossed in just three feeling words:

- Is this boundary something that has always been difficult for you to hold or is this a new challenge?

Boundary setting is a skill. Practicing can be tough because we usually don't spend much time intentionally working on our boundaries. This is a great spot to use visualization. Try this: Visualize yourself in a situation where you need to draw and hold your line. Now imagine that you have an invisible force field protecting you from being overrun. Your protection can look like whatever you like. I prefer to visualize the electric fence I had to open and close during my childhood chores of taking the horses and sheep in and out of the pasture. Many people find power in the image of a protective bubble. The trick is to use your imagination to make the protection strong. See those who would overrun you outside of the bubble, unharmed yet unable to encroach on your sovereignty. This is your realm, feel it. You are unafraid. Now, imagine they have made a request of you that crosses your boundaries. Reply—out loud—with your response. It doesn't need to be perfect. Just clearly state your no. You need not give an explanation. Just state your no.

When it comes time to set boundaries, having a plan is key. Since boundaries are invisible, focus on making them visible to you partner. Simply stating what you don't want is one way to make your boundary visible to your partner. It might feel a bit awkward at first, but it certainly feels better than not getting the kind of support you long for. Sandra brought her latest marketing graphics up on her phone and shared them excitedly with her partner. Unfortunately, Caden fell into his default mode of problem-solving. Since that's what he does all day at work, it feels natural. He jumps right into suggesting a tweak to the color and font size. Usually when this kind of thing happens, Sandra does her best to jam down her hurt feelings and just accept the unsolicited help because she wants to keep things positive. She likes that Caden is interested at all, so she tells herself she's just being overly sensitive.

That overly soft boundary led her to share less and less of the things she was excited about because she didn't want to fight. But setting boundaries isn't a fight, it is an invitation to know each other better. Sandra tried something different: "I think you want to help me, but you are offering critical feedback on my work when I really need a cheerleader right now." She said what wasn't working for her and let Caden know what she needed instead. To take this to the next level, the next time this kind of thing comes up she can make her request up front, saying something like, "I'm super excited about what I got done today. Would you help me stay pumped about this? I'm all set on feedback and I just need cheerleading for now, thanks." Clearly sharing boundaries at the outset of an interaction gives our partners a fair shot at meeting our expectations and stops a lot of bickering before it starts.

Action Step: Recognize Your Yes

One of the most challenging places to hold our boundaries is inside a love relationship. Some people were trained to have overly soft, pliable, removable, or even no boundaries when they are in a love situation. If this is you, it might be time to seek the help of a therapist or look into codependence group support.

If you struggle to hold only some of your boundaries, it might be that you simply aren't clear on your yeses, which makes it impossible to hold a strong no. For example, do you know what you like to do on an open weekend day? My partner struggles with this, quite intensely. For him, having a free weekend day is truly overwhelming—so many options, but which is the right one? To escape the overload, he often finds that he says yes to anything other people suggest. Without a clear yes of his own, he has no sense of when or how to say no in response to a request.

Step 1. Name a situation in which you struggle to know what you want. Maybe you feel stuck when your partner asks how you like to spend your "date night" time or how you want to spend a specific time of year. Many people, for example, struggle to define how they want to spend their holiday seasons. It could be any time you find you experience a fuzzy, unclear yes. Pick one example that happens to you frequently.

Step 2. Describe what a full yes would be like for you in this situation. Call to mind a really strong YES situation. You pick the weather, the style of approach your partner will bring, the way you are dressed. Every detail is just screaming HELL YEAH. Don't worry about how realistic the circumstance feels right now. Just let yourself feel the yes. Imagine it with every one of your senses.

Step 3. Now that you've got that full yes response going in your body, tune in. Really feel that yes. Where do you feel it, how do you feel it? Is the yes in your chest, your throat, is it a tingle everywhere? Stay with the yes until you feel it permeate your whole being. Remember this yes. This is your unique response to yes; it doesn't look like anyone else's. This is your full YES. Grab onto this sensation.

Key Takeaways

- Boundaries are a gift you give each other in a relationship.

- You might have a habit of letting your boundaries be overly soft or rigid. Reimagine boundaries to help your partner love you in ways that work for you.

- To set flexible, strong boundaries that you can communicate well, you need to know what you want and what you don't want.

- Learning how to identify what a full yes feels like will help you know where your boundaries are.

Chapter 4

Who Is This Person?

"I meant for this to be fun. I was just showing you how much I love you!" My husband really meant what he was saying—he did intend for us to have a fun evening. He'd planned for it too: He'd given me a gift to open earlier in the day, we'd gone out for dinner, and now we were alone and he was lightly rubbing my shoulders with one hand while he was fiddling with his phone to play some music. I lost it right around the third time he started a new song. In a voice strung so tight it almost snapped, I said "I think I'll go read something and go to sleep." It was barely seven o'clock. Ken looked at me with utter confusion. He thought he'd done everything right and here I was, clearly irritated and leaving the date he'd planned in a snit.

Once I'd gotten to my bedroom, I realized I had been grumpy all afternoon. What had started it? Why wasn't I happy that he was putting in all this effort? I felt like a brat and I didn't like anything about this sensation. When I noticed the present he'd given me sitting on my bureau, I realized that this whole day had felt "off" for me. I felt like I was supposed to be excited about the gift, the dinner, and the physical attention. Instead, all of it had frustrated me. This guy really does love me, but he had demonstrated love in ways that didn't show me that he <u>knew</u> me. He made a mistake that we all make sometimes: He tried to love me the way he wanted to be loved. Thankfully, once I recognized we were caught in this messy spot, I asked him for a do-over. He explained his intentions and I shared how I actually felt. The gift started us off on the wrong foot; I hate opening presents in front of people and we had company at the time he gave it to me. From there, we just kept missing each other's true desires. The do-over went much better. There were a lot more exploratory questions on both our parts and we found out that we actually had to give each other our metaphorical instruction book. With no more guessing, we started to be really clear about when, where, and how we want to be loved.

You can't love someone the way you want to be loved. It just doesn't work that way. Love is a verb in my book—to love someone means to act in loving ways. All too often, we do what we want and hope that our partner receives that action as love.

But we feel loved when we are seen exactly as we are and appreciated for it. In practical terms, that means we need to get to know each other and then actually act on what we know. This sounds simple enough. But more often than not, when a relationship isn't fun anymore, it's because we aren't loving each other as we are. We get caught up in a cycle of trying the same things over and over again, but if they aren't the things that make our partner feel loved, then who exactly are we doing them for? Chances are we are trying to love them the way we wish they were, not the way they are.

There is no getting around it. To know each other, we need to stay curious about this living, breathing, growing human we have committed to and learn how to love them the way they want to be loved. Why? Because anything less than that is about you. Self-love is awesome and utterly necessary, so shower yourself with it, please! But don't mistake the way you want to be treated for the way they do. We all want to be loved a bit differently.

Each of us came here wired up with certain predilections and preferences. Then we were raised by people who cared for us in ways that sometimes worked for us and that sometimes didn't. From this start as little children, we developed a set of expectations, a sort of unique-to-us love map. We like what feels familiar, even if it isn't the healthiest or most evolved version of love we can imagine. This doesn't mean that we can't make better choices than our childhood caregivers or that we are doomed to repeat the exact patterns of our parents. But, like it or not, we spent our earliest, most helpless years soaking up the patterns of love just the way they were presented. Loving is a practice, an action we choose, and we can definitely work on the unconscious desires that create cycles of feeling unloved or acting unlovingly.

But we cannot decide for someone else what love must look like. Bottom line: Your partner is an individual who has the right to feel loved in their own particular way. So do you!

This isn't super easy, and it isn't what most of us were taught about love. Most of us patterned our ideals about love from our earliest caregivers and then added details from trite movies and fairy tales with very little in the way of realistic mess-ups along the way. It's okay! None of us got an instruction book with all the answers to life.

The good news is that the hardest part about getting the love we desire is getting to know ourselves. Maybe that isn't a super-simple task, but it is worth the time. Depth psychologist C. G. Jung called this process individuation, which he described as a process of coming to wholeness through recognizing the diverse qualities we carry within. Like Jung, I believe we are all born whole, but that wholeness is innocent and undifferentiated. That type of wholeness is beautiful but lacks self-awareness and so while we are young, we are constantly learning about ourselves, becoming more and more ourselves. We don't benefit from trying to return to that innocent wholeness. Instead, we become a richer, more nuanced, mature, whole self, little by little.

Every day in childhood and adolescence, we find new facets of the world both within and outside of us. We are adventurers! But then for whatever reason, many people stop. They find a comfortable spot and stop exploring the complicated, fascinating mess of themselves. Becoming yourself is a process of looking inward. This can be disorienting for some folks and it takes time. But it is actionable work.

It can be hard to take a deep dive into the muck of your psyche while you are trying to build a life and a business. The trick is to bookmark the explorer within; re-engage with yourself as a wonder to behold. This might sound narcissistic, but that term is often misunderstood. The mythological Narcissus, who perished because he could not bear to look away from his beautiful self, is a warning we should all heed, but healthy self-interest is quite another thing. Don't fear getting to know yourself well.

When we turn our attention inward, sometimes our family and friends get scared. Sometimes they get angry or lash out because they feel abandoned. They have come to count on our willingness to set aside our deeper needs and attend to the outside world without self-regard. Sometimes this is so severe that when we try to learn about our inner self, the people who love us panic—they want things to stay as they are. Sometimes they recognize on a subtle level that our growth might mean we won't martyr ourselves to their needs anymore. Thank goodness, other people will recognize the spark of life you are fanning! Some folks will notice that you are becoming more interesting and more alive, even if they don't quite understand what you are doing.

The feeling that there was something more that I just HAD to explore swept into my life when I was 31. I had always been super curious, so at first I just thought I wanted a new career or hobby. I added the hardest exercise routines I could think of to my life. First a marathon (I'd never run before) and then, when completing the marathon partially tore my Achilles tendon, I started CrossFitting. I was still so restless. I had four kids under the age of ten, I ran our local homeschooling cooperative, I was always busy making new things, teaching kids, learning some new skill. But inside I felt hollow. I tried sharing this with my husband, but he just didn't understand. I had everything I said I wanted, why was I always so needy?

Looking back, what happened next seems almost predictable, but back then I didn't have the psychological vocabulary to name what I was feeling. My restlessness increased, my heart broke open, and my soul <u>demanded</u> attention.

So began my personal dark night of the soul. I wish I could tell you that it only lasted one night, but it was actually a couple of years. I wish I could say that I managed to do my soul work and learn who I really was without destroying any of my relationships, but sadly that just isn't true. I can tell you that I gained something utterly invaluable: I found ME inside all of the expectations and condemnations others had placed on me over the years. I emerged from my many dark nights as a more complicated, intricate version of my former self. I had access to parts of myself others had asked me to diminish by request or by force. Saying goodbye to friends and family who wished I never started my process of self-discovery was painful. I do miss them. But staying inside the lines pre-drawn for me was twisting my soul—it was emotional suicide. I love myself too much to squash myself in order to keep people who couldn't love me as I truly am.

As a woman, I used to think that loving myself that much must be pathological; I was trained to put myself last. I was wrong. Try it! Start practices that help you look at yourself the way you would look at a newborn child, with loving curiosity. You won't forget to care for others, you will just start caring for yourself equally.

Otherness

This section marks the transition from a focus on self-awareness to increasing your relational awareness. The beauty of this shift is that you will continue to learn about yourself as you deepen your ability to really know your partner. You might be hesitant at this point, maybe even wondering if you want to know that much more about your partner. Particularly if you are struggling in your relationship, it might feel like turning over too many rocks could just make the whole project too familiar and risk a boredom your commitment can't withstand. Don't panic.

Respected marriage therapist and author Esther Perel described the situation most clearly: Modern relationship is paradoxical. We want to be seen and known fully, to experience the kind of deep security that comes with a profound commitment. At the same time, we long for novelty, passion, for someone who doesn't have to love us to find us fascinating. How can we want both of these things? Because humans are freaking complicated. We feel multiple, opposed things all the time.

What I find most comforting when I think about this terrible paradox is that our partner isn't really the same from day to day, year to year anyways. We often lazily act as though they are known to us, but that growing, living creature by your side is always going to be something of a mystery. The trouble arises when we act as though we know them and in doing so we stop peeping into their dark corners and peering behind the curtains of their essential Otherness. I capitalize Other precisely because it is distinctly separate from you—like any proper noun or name might be.

Don't get me wrong, I think it is critical that everyone have some independent passions, in whatever form makes sense for each of you. Aligning every element of your lives with one single other person will likely lead to an enmeshed situation where neither of you is entirely yourself. Have your own hobbies, read interesting things to share your thoughts on, indulge your outside friendships. Trust me: You and your partner can spend a lifetime playing in the space between being entirely known and always in the process of becoming.

Communicating with Love

If you ask people who are really happy in their relationships about the secret behind their happiness, they will say something about communication. The thing is, though, that we can't be sure we know what they mean by communication. The communication pattern that fits one couple will likely feel all wrong to another. But a happy couple has a pattern of communication that works for them. This might sound a little scary, as if the magic formula for a happy marriage is unknowable because it is totally unique. Luckily, there are skills that underlie satisfying communication, so even though there is no single "correct" formula, there are plenty of practical steps to take to make your communication as solid as possible. Communication could take up an entire book of its own, but in this section, I want to hit the key skills and name the most dangerous pitfalls. Consider this a crash course in communication for love.

Communication is a skill most entrepreneurs rely on every day. Without great communication, how would anyone ever get your message? You probably CRUSH the communication game! Yet often the more skillful we are in our professional life, the more we let it slide at home. When I was designing wedding gowns for a living, I never once dressed in couture and went out. By the end of the day, I was tapped out and I didn't want to even look at a corset. It's also very different to communicate our entire soul to one person rather than craft a message that plays well in all time zones. In other words, even if you rock the communication game at work, it might take some thoughtful attention to transfer your communication skills into a format that supports intimate love. And though women are tasked with more responsibility for communication in this culture, that doesn't mean we are doing it well. Let's dive in and take a look at what communication for love is.

When we think about communication in our relationship, the tendency is to think about arguing. I care about arguing, but we are going to talk about that later. Right now, let's talk about communicating as a means to deepen intimacy, sharing our inner experience courageously and opening up to hearing and seeing our partner's inner world. What the heck is communication though? It's actually so broad it is hard to pin down. Communication comes in words, both verbal and written, in body language, touch, and subtle energetic sensations; it's all the ways we exchange our experience with another.

There are four key ingredients that make a solid foundation of loving communication:

- honoring individuality

- asking for what you need

- listening with care

- responding versus reacting

Let's consider how each of these looks in action.

Honoring Individuality

Honoring individuality probably seems a bit out of place. If we want to have better communication, why not just get down to brass tacks and talk about talking? Because you two almost certainly have different communication styles. Much like our personalities, our communication styles tend to be pretty stable over time but are not utterly concrete. I start with honoring individuality because it is so important to come to terms with the differences we have in communication. Without this step, we will be disappointed more often than not and over time we will turn away from each other more and more. We might lose the person we love more than anything because we make the mistake of assuming they can and will communicate the way we do.

One reason we fall into the trap of assuming our partner shares our communication style is because we just don't bother to imagine the wide variety in others. Maybe you have a basic idea about how you are different from your partner. My first husband and I certainly understood that we fell at the opposite ends of the talking spectrum: I used words, words, and more words; he often felt exhausted by words by lunchtime! But it wasn't just the sheer volume of words that separated us. Beyond that were many other differences that went unacknowledged, eventually leaving us both feeling unseen, misunderstood, and essentially unloved. This made for a really weak foundation, so it was all too easy for me to turn away from him when things got tough.

Though I don't regret our split—we've both remarried happily—I do regret the way we missed the chance to honor our differences rather than use them against each other.

Having trained in Jungian psychology, I find it easiest to imagine things in spectrums. Jung pictured a world made of polarities: dark and light, good and evil. Jung's view is a bit heavy handed on the idea that there are inherent opposites, but the energy that flows between any two things in relationship to each other, that energy is life. I say that to caution all of us—myself included—against positioning ourselves as opposite to our lovers (or anyone, really) when we consider our differences. In practical terms, just because I am a talker doesn't mean my partner is quiet. We aren't opposite ends of the full spectrum of talking versus silent; we just occupy different spots on a spectrum of chattiness. Some other common differences beyond number of words are speed of processing, cautiousness of word selection, willingness to self-disclose, need for privacy from others, and directness.

Assessment: Recognizing Individuality

Where do you fall on these spectrums?

I say lots of words.	I say few words.
I make rapid, spontaneous word selections.	I make cautious, careful word selections.
I quickly process thoughts and feelings into words.	I slowly process thoughts and feelings into words.
I will say anything I find in my inner world.	I tend to keep my inner world to myself.
I don't need privacy to share deeply.	I need assurances of privacy to share deeply.
I state things quite directly.	I use ambiguous language regularly.
I process things by talking.	I process things inside before sharing.

Assessment: Love Languages

Asking for what you want is a million times harder if you don't know what you want. When it comes to feeling loved, it is pretty easy to think that our partner should just "get" us. Songs, movies, novels—stories everywhere tell us that true love is intuitive and "natural." Yeah, that's just not how life works.

The best method I've come across for making your love map obvious is the Five Love Languages, a succinct system developed by Gary Chapman. See www.5lovelanguages.com to get a handle on your love languages with a quick questionnaire. Chapman established five general categories of giving and receiving love: words of affirmation, acts of service, gifts, quality time, and touch. Before you take the questionnaire, I would like to draw your attention to the final category: touch. When considering the love language of touch, I would encourage you to think about a variety of kinds of touch. Touch comes in many forms, and while sex is one of them, it certainly isn't the only important touch in love relationships. There is a danger of conflating sex and touch in the love languages quiz, especially if you and your partner experience a desire mismatch (wanting sex in different amounts). If touch comes up as one of your (or your partner's) top two love languages, I encourage you to explore more deeply what you actually mean by touch. The Define Sex action step in Chapter 8 is going to be particularly important for you if touch ranks high for you or your partner.

Asking for What You Need

This is a tricky bit of communication. To be able to ask for what you need, first you need to know what the heck you need. If you aren't clear on your needs yet, don't be surprised when things in your relationship aren't going the way you want. This isn't bad news, because it actually means you still have a chance to get the love you want—you just haven't really asked for it yet. The assessments and action steps throughout this book are designed for exactly this purpose—to help you know who you are and what you want. But knowing isn't enough. You must find a way to get your message across. Unfortunately, this isn't always as simple as just saying the words, but that is where the process begins! When you want to make a change at work, you know you have to communicate that change. Your partner is no different. Learning how to actually say the thing— name your need <u>out loud</u>—is critical. In Chapter 7, we will explore how to communicate your need explicitly.

Listening with Care

Being heard is not the same thing as being understood. I find this distinction important because sometimes we want to be heard and it doesn't really matter if our listener understands us. When I am practicing a speech, I don't mind if my audience is my 11-year-old and the topic is synchronicity. In this case, I just need someone to hear my words and let me practice eye contact. Venting is another instance. It's enough sometimes just to have a chance to tell someone what is bothering you. But when it comes to communicating with our partner, there is usually a desire to be understood. This requires a sort of attentive listening that doesn't come naturally for everyone.

Stepping up your listening game starts with asking a question of the speaker: What kind of listening do you need right now? Do you need me to listen with quiet support or do you need me to engage with you actively, asking questions to clarify as you go along? Take the guesswork out of the process by asking. Sometimes we don't know what kind of listening we need or our needs change as we talk, but since a simple question can increase our success, get in the habit of asking.

Responding in Place of Reacting

Once you've established that you want some engaged listening, there is one remaining skill to master so the communication train doesn't come off the rails. We humans are just not very far removed from our animal selves, especially when we are activated by anger, grief, jealousy, or other strong emotions. When we are in this activated state, it is all too easy to react without reflection. This is almost always a less-than-optimal outcome because our initial reactiveness doesn't tend to mesh very well with our partner's need to be understood.

The trick to responding is to s-l-o-w d-o-w-n. Literally, slow everything down, especially if you are having an emotional reaction to what you are hearing.

This is a magic moment. I really, really wish it weren't this. I personally process and act very quickly. I like that about myself. I'm decisive and up tempo. And for all the good that does me in some areas, when it comes to reactive behavior, being naturally quick is no help at all. Learning to slow down my reaction was the only way to stop pushing other people (especially more patient or reserved people) out of my life or up the walls. It doesn't matter that slowing down doesn't come naturally, it only matters that it works. Slowing down increases my chances of staying connected and responding with care.

It looks like this: Take a few deep breaths. (Don't roll your eyes while you are doing this. Close them if needed.) Let your prefrontal cortex—the part of your brain that is capable of rational problem-solving—come online before responding to the words you are hearing. Then, use "I" statements: I feel, I notice, I need, I love. Stick to your side of the street by claiming only what is true for you. Don't put words in the other person's mouth, and don't assume you know how they are feeling. Assume goodwill on your partner's part. The goal is to be seen and heard authentically and to respond to what is actually going on.

Michelle learned quickly that even if she was intending to listen, it was absolutely imperative that she slow herself down when she and Chris were talking about anything important. If the topic got too close to her sore spots, it was too easy to slip into her old habit of cracking sarcastic jokes. Then Chris would default to a pouty silence, and before they knew what happened they were on opposite sides of a battle rather than having a meaningful discussion. Their goal was to learn about each other and make space for their differences, but the temptation to react from their less mature sides was overwhelming. Michelle made a big change by deciding to take five slow, even breaths before she responded during conversations about anything even a little bit uncomfortable. It was a small change in the scheme of things, just a few seconds really, but those seconds bought Michelle time to respond to Chris with genuine curiosity. This time gave her the chance to be herself again and to move toward Chris, even if they didn't agree on the topic at hand.

If you are feeling intense emotions, it is reasonable to need to take a bigger break than five breaths. Maybe you need to take a walk to cool down. One caveat though: If you need to take a break, tell your partner when you will come back and talk about the issue. Without this reassurance, your partner may feel abandoned or alone. Schedule a time to come back together. Together you can face the emotions, but it's okay to need some time to let your instinctual reactiveness pass. Slowing down gives you time to make "I" statements and speak from a place of love and caring negotiation. This is how you can change a reactive, volatile tone into one of generosity and response.

Key Takeaways

- Love is a verb. Your actions create a loving relationship whether you mean them to or not.

- To love someone well, we need to recognize how they <u>receive</u> love. Don't just assume you know. It is super common to try to love others the way we like to be loved.

- Communication in relationships rests on four pillars: honoring individuality, asking for what you need, listening with care, and responding versus reacting.

- Responding rather than reacting takes slowing down, but it increases connection even during times of stress. Slow down, take a few breaths, monitor for aggressive body language like eye rolling and crossed arms.

- If you need to walk away to cool down (and chill that reactive brain), tell your partner when you will be willing to talk about this issue again.

Chapter 5

Relationship Resilience

Going big in your relationship means taking some risks. We are going to be sharing new parts of ourselves, trying things that might feel uncomfortable, and having courageous conversations. Building some resilience up front is the best way to ease the growing pains. Resilience isn't a concrete thing. Relationship resilience is about creating an environment of supportive and flexible responsiveness.

The ingredients of resilience can and should be custom crafted for your relationship. Everyone's day looks different. You might have synchronized schedules that allow for a shared bedtime, or you may work late every evening while your partner gets up before sunrise to catch the early train into the city. Some people work in the same space with their partner all day long, others are happy having their together time mostly on weekends. There is no perfect recipe. Togetherness is defined by the people in the relationship.

Maybe you don't have to have loads and loads of time together, but you can still find a way to connect deeply.

Time is not the only way to go deep, but if you have less time you will need to develop an ability to get present and vulnerable intentionally, without investing tons of hours. Honestly, reconnection takes some intentionality even if you do drop into vulnerable spaces easily. Humans tend to have trouble with transitions. Don't feel bad about it, just learn to work with the fact. We get into our groove, and then it's tough to pull ourselves out of that mode and participate in the next. When I was a kid, my parents called their transition time after work "coffee time." It was sacred. If you were a kid, you were either quietly pleasant or you left the room while they decompressed together for 45 minutes at the end of their workdays. They both had physically demanding jobs, and this was a necessary element of their relationship. Seriously, my brother and I knew not to mess with those two and that pot of coffee. It wasn't until I was an adult working a retail schedule while my husband had a night job that I truly appreciated what my mom and dad were doing during coffee time. It was never about the coffee, of course. It was their reconnection—the time when the two of them reminded themselves of why they worked hard and what it was worth.

Tool: Building Ritual Template

The importance of ritual in our lives cannot be overstated. It doesn't need to be complicated or cost a thing. Ritual grounds us and creates a sacred space, a *temenos*, for reconnection, learning, and love. Rituals can be made to fit any time and space. They are the fingerprint of your relationship. Creating rituals that work for you is a game changer. Rather than focusing on what doesn't work in your relationship, the effort here is on making fun little changes that add up to big happiness.

I use the word "ritual" because creating the loving relationships we long for is sacred work. More than just a healthy habit, a ritual is a practice that nurtures the soul as well as the body and brain. Rituals aren't work, and they don't need to be rare. Our relationship rituals are things we do to enjoy our time together. We call them rituals so that we remember how sacred those little moments of joy together really are.

Here is my simple formula for creating rituals that encourage you to practice love as action every day:

Time + Kindness + Particularity = Our Ritual

Put a little less succinctly, the formula looks like this: <u>When</u> do we do this thing? + <u>How</u> do we do this thing? + <u>What</u> do each of us need for this ritual to suit our unique personalities?

The ritual formula was made to help you create custom experiences that fit you and your partner just right. By putting a bit of energy into consciously designing your unique rituals, you can shift areas of life that have become stale and routine. Investing in intentional rituals of reconnection is the master tool that constantly supports your individual growth and the strength of your relationship.

Action Step: Building Ritual

Step 1. Start small. Pick something to do that is not scary or upsetting for either of you.

Step 2. Reduce friction. Choose something with low barriers to adherence. In other words, choose something that won't stretch your budget or schedules. Simple is best.

Step 3. Choose a known quantity. Take something you already do together and make it a regular thing.

Step 4. Make it stick. New habits need a trigger. Use the when/then technique below to avoid slippery words that make it easy to back out of a ritual "just this one time." Pick a day and time for this ritual and set your alarms now. Put it on your shared calendar. Write it on the fridge. Fill in and repeat the sentence below to each other:

When it is _____(fill in day and time),
we will be _____ (fill in the activity).

Examples:

When it is 4 PM Thursday, we will be at the coffee shop having a latte and spending an hour device-free with each other.

When it is 9 PM on Friday, we will be in bed reading poetry to each other. (Okay, I know this one makes it sound like I am really sappy but try it. I never knew how much I could enjoy poetry until I started sharing it out loud with a lover.)

Time	+ Kindness	+ Particularity	= Our Ritual
When do we do this? What triggers our ritual?	How do we do this? What is our intention?	What do we do? Make it reflect what you two enjoy!	Be creative and welcome simplicity. The goal is little, specific rituals done regularly.
Example:			
Alarm goes off at 6 AM but one of us is headed to the shower and one to workout.	Connection and presence is our goal	A five-minute snuggle and some eye contact before either of us touches our phones.	We found that we fall back asleep easily, but we like the connection. So now we sit up in bed and snuggle. Still no phones.

In the table above, you can see one example of a little ritual created by a couple using the formula. The particularity part is especially important. This ritual serves the two of you, so let it be as weird as you want! At the end of his workday, Tom comes into the kitchen and puts on a playlist of music he and Zia both like. She is usually still working in the office located off the kitchen, so the music is a gentle signal that Tom is home and ready to connect. Still, it doesn't require her to stop her workflow mid-sentence. Tom used to greet Zia with a kiss and conversation as soon as he got home; you can imagine his surprise when he found out that his very loving intention was actually driving her nuts. Zia would feel pressured to be ready to stop her thoughts at a moment's notice and traffic meant that moment could be anytime between 5 PM and 5:45 PM. It killed her productivity in that last hour. The shift to a ritual of music gives her the time she needs to transition. On her end, she is committed to coming out of the office within two songs; one is usually plenty to wrap things up though, so that she feels understood. A kiss is the next step, and Tom has recently added some tea to the ritual. He pops the water onto the stove during those transitional minutes. The trick is to try some rituals out and tweak them to fit you!

Living with Each Other

Whether you've been living together for years or you are just moving in, the physical intimacy of sharing living space comes with challenges. Of course, it also comes with great rewards. The willingness to share our mundane existence with another human being is a gift. We tend to focus on the early days of a love story: the meetup, the first kiss, the first date. We worry about that second date: will they ask us, will we get a yes, will we fall in love. Philosopher Alain de Botton said: "Love stories begin not when we fear someone may be unwilling to see us again but when they decide they would have no objection to seeing us all the time." I just love how he put that. Remembering the sparks of first love serves a purpose, sure. But the decision to live with someone is a different statement altogether: This person is someone I want to see every day, someone I want to spend time with when they are sick, sad, even angry. I want to laugh with this person as we grow older and our bodies fall apart. I want to see their weird self in all its permutations.

To be clear, I don't think living together is a requirement for deep intimacy or true love. You can be fully committed and choose to live alone, designing your relationship in a way that best suits you and your partner. But this chapter is for those who make the choice to live together, sharing bathrooms and bills, navigating boredom and bad habits on a daily basis. Living together makes us vulnerable in some specific ways that deserve attention.

Sometimes we make a choice and never revisit our motivation for that choice. Living together is often that kind of decision. At some point, we decided to move in together. Maybe it was a practical decision, like sharing expenses or one of us getting to move closer to work. Perhaps it was a spontaneous, exciting decision brought on by a flash of impetuously fresh love. There isn't a right or wrong way to decide. When I was first moving in with my now husband, let's just say it was super complicated. Sometimes I would wonder what the heck I was doing. Over the next few years, I was unsure an awful lot, often wondering if we would have fewer problems if we lived separately. More than a decade later, I realize that the day I figured out my "why" for living with this person was the day everything started to make more sense. Figuring out why I live with him gave me an opportunity to be really, deeply grateful for the choice I made every day. It's the feeling of gratitude that will buoy you through the annoyances of living together. Gratitude is the only antidote I know of for the sound of snoring, socks on the floor (again), or closet space cramped by someone else's shoe collection.

Assessment: My Relationship "Why"

Remember the original spark that caught your interest in this person you share a life with? Well, now that you've spent time with them and the sparkliness may have worn away, it's a good time to look into your motivations for sticking with this lovely human. I suggest that you both do this if at all possible. Knowing why you are "us" makes it possible to open your eyes each day actually looking forward to the nuts and bolts of making a life together.

- Why do you live here, in this place, with this person?

- Name one thing your partner does that makes your life sparkle:

- Name one thing you do that brings a smile to your partner's face:

- Where would you be if you weren't with this person?

- Name three things you are grateful for in your life tied to your partner:

If you don't remember any reasons why or you have nothing good to say about your partner, NOW is the time to work with a therapist or coach one-on-one. Don't wait another minute. Every marriage counselor I have ever met (and that is a LOT of people) remarks that couples almost always wait too long to seek out help. Getting a little outside, professional perspective on your relationship can make a difference you can't yet imagine.

Chances are you found plenty to be grateful for in your partnered life. This is your "why." You are going to lean on it during those moments when the going gets tough. You will use it to clarify choices that seem ambiguous and murky. Hang your "why" on your fridge or somewhere you'll both see every day.

Sore Spots

When we share our living space, it is pretty easy to find areas of life that we just do not agree upon. There are some things that are deal-breakers: those kinds of things that are just plain NOT alright with you on an ethical level, the kind of thing that ended some earlier relationships or that stopped you from swiping right on tons of profiles. This exercise isn't designed to get you reconsidering your deal-breaker hard-line. There is another kind of disagreement, though, that can wear away at your happiness without being a full-on deal-breaker. I like to call these sorts of problems sore spots. The two of you aren't harming yourselves or others, but boy oh boy do these problems chafe. They start off just rubbing the wrong way, but over time they can leave you feeling raw.

In my first marriage, one of our sore spots involved touch. We had vastly different needs for touch in all forms. It didn't seem too big a deal at first, but over the years it became a huge tension point. These sorts of discrepancies often seem manageable at the beginning of a relationship. You love going to drum circles, you feel at home there and can't imagine your life without them. Your lover is passionate about gaming, it's more than just a hobby, it really fills a need for them. In those first months, it's all cool. Having separate interests is part of what makes life interesting. And that's still true today, except somehow you keep feeling like they don't care about this thing that really matters to you. They don't understand why you are frustrated at the amount of time and money they feel is appropriate for their passion project.

Maybe it has become even stickier. Perhaps you love your church and want to have your newborn daughter dedicated, but your partner just can't see eye to eye with you. They didn't mind your being gone Sunday mornings or sharing coffee while you chatted about your Bible group, but they just don't want to go down that route with their children. Or perhaps the difference really becomes a pain in the butt over time. Before you lived together, it was almost unnoticeable but now the resentment is seeping into your bedroom and hanging out at the kitchen table.

The point is, living together adds many layers of complexity to your relational life. If you aren't in a deal-breaker situation (when it is definitely time to either end the relationship or seek significant therapeutic intervention), what do you do with these sore spots?

Assessment: Noticing Your Sore Spots

Name the sore spot. Get super specific: what hurts, what's missing, what act is causing constant tension?

- What would life look like if this situation were exactly as you wished?

- What need in you is not being met?

- Is this a need you can get met elsewhere without breaking your relationship agreements?

Now that you've identified these sore spots, let's look at what might bring these tough experiences to the surface in your relationship.

Emotional Labor

No relationship book fit for the 21st century should leave out a discussion about emotional labor. It doesn't get talked about nearly enough. Emotional labor in the context of a household is the collection of tasks no one gets paid for but that someone has to do in order for life to carry on the way we've come to expect. Many of these tasks are laden with emotional overtones, hence the name emotional labor. Sometimes I wish we could change the name though, because emotional labor includes plenty of physical work and has a far deeper impact than it sounds like. Emotional labor includes tasks like keeping track of various family calendars, lining up who brings cupcakes and who brings booze to the next party, where the luggage should get stored when you've run out of closet space, how to get your aging family member to their doctor's appointment during the middle of a workday, talking your partner down after a crappy day, and a million other tasks large and small. This type of work is imbalanced in most relationships, with one partner taking on the lion's share of these invisible tasks. In heterosexual relationships, the load is more frequently borne by the woman and it is almost never recognized fully.

If your relationship is balanced, or you've found a split that really works for both of you, awesome! I send you the highest of high fives! Be proud, but don't be complacent. That feeling of balance takes some effort to maintain over the course of a relationship because we change. Our needs and the needs of the household change. Keep an eye on it.

If your relationship is obviously imbalanced, well, you aren't alone. This isn't going to go away by ignoring the issue or by posting a thousand hashtags about self-care. We also won't make any headway if we blame our partner for the problem and don't actually prioritize changing the situation.

That's right—and it sucks. In order to get some balanced emotional labor going on in our households, we are going to have to invest some emotional labor. It's the paradox of our times, and we are just going to have to boss up on this one. On a societal level, I'm committed to relieving the pressure by working directly with the biggest power-holding demographic in our country—white men—to help them recognize and shift their emotional labor attitudes. They can use the help, and I love working with guys. I really do believe that they want to deal with this problem. But that's another book.

Right now though, I'm only concerned with helping you make this change in your life, starting today. Finding your way out of a labyrinth of emotional labor is one small step in creating a world where we are all caregivers and care receivers. Today, start with what you have control over: your own thoughts, feelings, and actions.

It's time to take a look at where we are supporting the continuation of the emotional labor imbalance. It might be that we have higher standards than our partners or that we can't stand their timing issues or that they learned the trick of doing something poorly so they wouldn't be asked again. It doesn't matter what the cause is on their end, though. What we can do is get our act together and stop pulling on our end of the tug-of-war.

Assessment: What Really Matters?

Step 1. Make a list of some of the tasks you do that your partner takes for granted:

- Do these tasks come up in the arguments you have with your partner?

- Do you feel irritated by these tasks, maybe like a pebble in your shoe, even if you choose not to argue about them?

Step 2. Does it feel like your partner is not doing their share of the emotional/invisible labor?

- What does it feel like in your body right now, thinking about how they react to these unseen jobs? Do you feel tightness, buzzing, constriction, swirling, vibrating, nausea, heat, numbness?

- Do the jobs you've listed really need to be done? Get real with yourself. Who are you doing these things for? If you removed half of these tasks, what would happen? Are any of these tasks done because of how you want other people to see you?

Step 3. Make a list of invisible tasks you believe should not be your job, but you absolutely believe need to be done. You can use this list along with the Explicit Agreements Template you will find in Chapter 7 to design an explicit agreement with your partner about who will do these tasks.

Step 4. This is the MAGIC step. Do not skip it! Here it is: You must, absolutely must, allow your partner to do the jobs in their own way. Yes, it will not be done the way you did it. Sometimes it will go badly. This is what it means to treat your partner as an autonomous adult.

Letting Go

Of course, you will have priorities and core values that you won't let go of. But everything cannot be equally weighed. How the recycle gets sorted can't get the same level of attention as making your childcare decisions or choosing what state to live in. Without prioritization, you are going to drown in unimportant but tantalizingly urgent crud. You'll miss out on living your best life if you don't prioritize. It's exactly the same in business, right?

Thankfully, you have a superpower to use here: your imagination. Your life is whatever you can imagine. It isn't limited to what you're already doing. To get the life you want, including support in all this invisible work, what must be reimagined? You might lower your standard about a particular task, let go of something following your specific timeline, or let go entirely of a job that your partner does completely differently from you. Reimagining is a life-giving action. Take a deep breath and imagine yourself like Elsa from the Disney movie *Frozen*, letting go of all kinds of urgent-feeling BS that is currently keeping you from your most important work.

Respect and Role Clarity

Now that we've started to untangle you from taking responsibility for every task in the world, it's time to use an even bigger tool to make life easeful and loving: role clarity.

Each of us has a unique ecosystem of home, self, love, and work. A few things in your life are entirely, 100 percent yours, where no one else is involved at any level of decision-making. In some spots, your interests overlap with those of your lover, your family, your friends, your employees, and your larger community. If you happen to own a business with a romantic partner, the overlap of domains is even higher. If you have kids and own a business, the overlap is higher still. If you sat down determined to make a chart outlining all the relationships between all the decision makers and influencers in all aspects of your life, it would quickly look unmanageable. But interconnection is highly valuable, and walling yourself off from others isn't practical. I could even make a case that high levels of isolation are detrimental to your well-being, not that I haven't been tempted myself. The complications of running multiple business ventures, raising seven kids, and getting my PhD all at the same time can create a desire do everything myself, even as a fairly extroverted person, walling off from anyone else just for simplicity's sake. Tempting, yes, and also a recipe for major burnout.

The trick to simplifying without isolating yourself or overburdening one person (often you, right?) is to get clear on the roles we each hold. Role clarity is such a valuable tool and so often overlooked in our personal life. At work, we don't hire someone until we have a job description, right? When you volunteer with an organization that matters to you, the first thing you do is choose a role that actually fits your abilities and schedule. You might choose a role that stretches your current capabilities—no one grows without stretching. But when I wanted to volunteer at a local hospital, I didn't offer to handle surgery; I offered to design a product that would help their patients (at the time, I was a fashion design student). Role clarity can't be beat when it comes to avoiding burnout.

The most effective way to use role clarity in your relationship is to make it a team activity. Getting buy-in from a partner is not the same as getting buy-in from someone you pay to show up every day, obviously. Holing up by yourself, making a big ole chore chart, and assigning tasks might seem like the expedient route but it also undermines the autonomy of the other people in your life. The next exercise is designed to help you name the domains in your world. Get them written down, together. This is one of the longer processes in the book and it is worth your time.

Action Step: Who's Responsible?

Partnered if possible

This step takes an hour or more, but you don't have to do it in one fell swoop. Get it started and you can revisit. Don't try to get it perfectly complete; it will change over time anyway. Perfection will stop you from putting this action step to use today. You can use paper and pencil, a big white board, or nerd-out with a shared spreadsheet like I do with my partner. The spreadsheet is what got his buy-in, honestly. Choose something you can use easily right out of the gate. Don't bog yourself down with technology if that's not your thing.

Step 1. List all the <u>domains</u> of home life that need consistent management, like:

Home, inside

Home, outside

Money

Kids

Food

Pets

Extended family

Volunteer commitments

Avocations (unpaid, meaningful hobbies and projects)

Step 2. List all the tasks you can think of under each domain. Don't get too fiddly; you can add to this list over time, but do spend enough time to assess each area. Pay close attention to tasks that need doing on a regular basis, especially daily and weekly. Often, we see a split of tasks where one partner takes responsibility for the infrequent tasks while the other has responsibility for the ongoing tasks. This split can wind up feeling bad in an invisible way: Those daily tasks add up quickly and frequently require keeping a lot of details in mind at all times. Think managing calendars, making appointments, planning, buying, and packing lunches—those sorts of tasks.

Sample Worksheet for Role Clarity

This sample is just a small chunk of a worksheet done recently by a client. They found several things that they both felt responsible for and a couple that neither of them wanted to do. This gave them a starting point to discuss what changes were needed to get rid of tasks they can't stand and to stop the daily passive-aggressive jabs they were both making about jobs no one had really taken responsibility for.

	Home, Inside		Home, Outside		Kids		Money		Food		Extended Family	
	Task	Who	Task	Who	Task	Who	Task	Who	Task	Who	Task	Who
	Dishes	Kids	Trash & recycle	Kids	Managing calendar	Zia	Bill paying	Zia	Meal planning	Zia	Negotiating holiday visits	Tom
	Vacuuming	Kids	Snow removal	Tom "(Can we shift to paid removal?)	Find seasonal clothing	Zia	Vacuuming	Zia	Grocery shopping	Tom	Phone check-ins with grandma	Tom
	Wiping counters	Kids	Walk the dog	Tom AM Zia midday Tom & Zia PM	Homework help	Tom	Wiping counters	Tom	Cooking dinner	Tom & Zia	Make food for gatherings	Zia
	Organizing storage	Zia & Tom	Get the mail	anyone	Oversee chores	Tom	Organizing storage	Tom	Planning & Packing lunch	Tom	Manage hurt feelings	Tom & Zia

Seeing Your Relationship Ecosystem

Now that you have a physical image of your relationship ecosystem, let's look at who is in that system. Do you have a business that brings employees into your home? Do you live with roommates, chosen family, or aging parents? Do you have kids? Everyone will have some roles and responsibilities. For this exercise, you are going to focus on who is responsible for making sure a particular area is well cared for, whether the work is delegated or done personally.

Only you can decide what makes for an easeful home life. In my relationship ecosystem, I have held many different roles, though it's pretty easy to see the roles that tend to fall into my realm. I prefer organizing to cleaning, for instance, so I tend to have the quarterly and yearly big jobs around the house while other members do the daily dishes. The goal is to get clear about responsibility and to be able to show gratitude to each other for all of our contributions. It takes a lot of kinds of effort to make this life work.

Key Takeaways

- Build resilience in your relationship to make your Project Relationship experience feel less risky.

- Small, daily rituals increase your relationship's ability to bounce back from the ups and downs of modern life and aid you in being vulnerable with each other.

- Connection works best if it is practiced in little ways all the time.

- Emotional labor (and the very physical labor that accompanies it) is often unbalanced in our households. Take stock of all that it takes to keep your world going 'round.

- Establish role clarity in your household. Get clear on who is responsible for what and make it explicit.

- When your partner has taken responsibility for something, let go of it needing to be handled your way and respect their ownership of the task.

Chapter 6

Courageous Connecting

Entrepreneurs understand that tolerating risk is part of the game. You don't play everything super safe; you know that in order to create a business, you have to risk wisely. When you choose a location, your product, or the market you want to enter, you assess the situation and then take action. That doesn't mean everything goes perfectly. But, if you don't risk starting you won't have a business at all. You stick your neck out knowing that success begins with ACTION. The same principle holds for relationships. We fall into a pattern with our partner pretty quickly, which feels good at first. We settle into our routine. That routine can make it hard to tell your partner what you really need, especially if your needs have changed or you didn't know how to share them right at the start.

Connecting courageously is a risk worth taking. Your partner can't know you unless you invite them into your full catastrophe. Inviting them in doesn't make them responsible for fixing your messes. It doesn't mean they will share all of your desires. In fact, it's pretty unlikely that everything will overlap. That's great! The differences between you two are exactly what creates the space for passion in your life. But we'll get to the passion in a little bit. For now, let's figure out what it means to let yourself be loved.

It might be very difficult to tell your partner how you prefer to be loved. Perhaps you don't know how they will react to your true desires. Or, maybe you feel selfish or narcissistic just talking about your needs. You may have been trained by former partners or caregivers that having any needs of your own is a violation of the unspoken agreements that make your relationship. They were just passing along their own misunderstanding of love, but it might have left you feeling frozen and incapable of being direct even today.

Don't panic. This is a great investment. The benefits far outweigh the risk. You do hard things all the time in the name of business. You take action in the face of fear. This is a transferable skill. You can retrain yourself.

Our lovers should never be expected to read our minds, nor us theirs. It isn't more romantic to have everything happen spontaneously—that is a trope from a bad rom-com. Romance—sexy, passionate, mouth-watering romance—grows from the fertile ground of sharing our deepest desires explicitly. That's right, you are going to find a way to tell your partner exactly how you feel most loved, in real, out-loud WORDS.

For those who just got freaked out: Don't worry too much. There are action steps that involve no spoken words at all. This process can be a gradual, gentle experience, not just a shocking jump into the deep end of your vulnerability.

For those who are thinking, I already tell my partner everything—great! There is probably more though. You picked up this book for a reason. Maybe you do share well, and these action steps will deepen that habit. Maybe there are parts of you that you hide even from yourself that could come out to play. Or perhaps you have more work to do in listening to and incorporating the real desires of your partner. This has been my experience.

I thought I was sharing myself for years when I had a breakthrough which—surprise, surprise—looked suspiciously like a breakdown. I hadn't realized that my great, big boldness—my willingness to (ostensibly) "say anything"—was masking something important. I was sharing, but it turned out I was only sharing within certain boundaries. This was hidden from me because I had mistaken the persona I wore for my personality, and even for my whole self. The word *persona* comes from the Greek word for mask. Personas are great places to hide because they often look and sound like a real, whole person. But a persona isn't the whole you. My persona wasn't the whole me. The mask I was wearing had become a full-body costume that was so close to real I even fooled myself some days. My role allowed me to own a set of qualities that I loved: clear thinking, honest, powerful, decisive, bold. It also assigned me negative qualities I didn't like so much: uncaring, unkind, brash. But the problem wasn't the persona itself. Honestly, it served a purpose. With that persona on, I accomplished big, bold things! The problem was in mistaking that persona for my true self. My whole self includes kind, gentle, shy parts. I am both brash and gentle, yes. What mysterious aspects are hiding within you?

Assessment: Unmasking Your True Self

- How do you mistake your persona (the mask you need to wear to get by in many public spaces and superficial relationships) for your wholeness?

- How do you limit yourself by believing your costume is all that you are? (If this feels impossible, imagine what a close friend would say are your best qualities—or actually ask them!)

- Do you hide away some parts of yourself, unable to give life to them because they have been tucked away so long?

Practicing the Magic of Curiosity

The other side of this coin is that you need to get to know what your partner really desires if you want to love them well. There is one, simple but astonishingly underutilized trick for this: Ask them. Ask them questions about themselves as a child. Ask them to tell you stories from their day. Ask them their favorite color, the time of day that they absolutely love, their most cherished memory of your life together. Ask them what they trust, and why. Ask them how they would spend a perfect day.

Ask your partner questions <u>as if you didn't already know the answer</u>. Even if you think you do know the answer, you are creating a new possibility just by opening up and being curious. Treat your partner as if they were a brand new, never-before-seen treasure and they may just surprise you. In fact, invite them to surprise you! Sometimes we fall into the habit of telling people what we think they expect to hear. Dare to explore without that expectation.

The next exercise is more than a one-off thing. It is the beginning of a lifetime of nurturing that magical feeling of seeing and being seen by each other. When I work with couples, I'm often stunned to find that they assume that they know their partner completely. Face it, they came to see me because something wasn't working very well, so why would they assume they know everything about each other? It's a pretty hopeless stance to take. Assuming you know someone leaves out a critical piece of the human equation: We grow and change all the time. Change is normal! Sure, many things are stable. My mother's favorite color was blue from the time she was five years old until she died. My tendency to process my thoughts out loud has been with me since I was little. But many things shift and lots more are never even known consciously until someone asks us!

Taking the time to ask each other questions was even put forth as a science-meets-magic formula for making two people fall in love in a popular *New York Times* article by Mandy Len Catron, building off the psychological research of Dr. Arthur Aron. The premise of the article was that by taking two people and having them ask each other a series of increasingly personal questions followed by an eye-gazing experience, anyone could potentially experience what we commonly call "falling in love." I don't really care how scientific this particular practice is though, because I have put it to the test and I have seen it change lives. I don't mean I've been asking strangers to fall for each other; I mean that when I am working with folks who are struggling to find the passion they once had, I find this practice just works. By engaging in intimate, vulnerable, and fun exploration together, we can hold the tension of Otherness alongside the joy of security. And that is as close to a magic spell as I've ever found.

Action Step: The Curiosity Date

The point isn't to "get through" these questions. The point is to use this list to get back in the habit of seeing your partner as multifaceted and interesting. You might plan a long getaway date and go through the whole list, but personally I've never gotten through more than a couple dozen questions before my partner and I are sharing other stories, off on a tangent of deep sharing sparked by one question or another. Ask follow-up questions, wander down unmarked paths. Just make sure to switch back and forth. Often one partner is more comfortable talking than the other. The talker may be used to filling up all the verbal space. If this is one of you, one way for the quieter person to have a bit more time to find their words is to use a physical object (I like a smooth rock) to pass back and forth. Only the person holding the rock is answering the question at that moment. As a talker, I love this physical reminder to make a little room for my partner!

This is a great activity when sitting together somewhere cozy, but it also works well on a walk, over dinner, or even hanging out waiting in line somewhere (obviously, you'll have to choose the questions more selectively in a more public setting).

1. What was your favorite story as a child?
2. What's your favorite color?
3. When was the first time you went swimming in your life?
4. Who is your role model for a happy relationship?
5. What kind of weather makes you want to go outside?
6. What time of day do you feel most sexual?
7. Have you ever stayed up all night? Tell me what kept you up?

8. If you could have any job, what would you do?
9. Where were you the first time you felt amazed by the beauty of the world?
10. What's your idea of a perfect day off?
11. If you could travel anywhere today, where would you go?
12. What subject did you enjoy most in eighth grade?
13. If you could have one more conversation with someone who is gone now, who would it be and what would you talk about?
14. What do you wish you could change about the world, right now?
15. What do you struggle with when you travel alone?
16. What memory stands out the most from your 20s?
17. Can you touch your nose with your tongue, wiggle your ears, or make a funny face I don't know about?
18. What hobby do you wish you had taken up as a child?
19. Did you ever go somewhere and get totally lost? What happened?
20. What is the farthest you've traveled alone?
21. What was your favorite song last year?
22. Would you dance on stage if you were pulled up there by your favorite musician?
23. What is your dream job or business?
24. What book would you say is a must-read?
25. What is your biggest pet peeve?
26. Are you missing anyone right now?
27. Do you get jealous easily?

28. What color was your childhood room painted?
29. What's your favorite dessert?
30. Do you like a good cry?
31. Would you rather be in a summer rainstorm or winter snowstorm?
32. Did you have any cute nicknames as a child?
33. What's your secret superpower?
34. If all of your clothes had to be one color, what would you choose?
35. What's your favorite memory of your family of origin?
36. What's your least favorite memory of your family of origin?
37. Do you want any pets you don't already have?
38. Have you ever gone swimming in the open ocean? Is it fun or scary to you?
39. What's your favorite myth or fairy tale?
40. If you could change one thing about this world, what would it be?
41. If you could be immortal, would you?
42. Would you ever consider going on a reality television show?
43. Have you ever been on a rooftop?
44. If you could change one of your habits, which one would it be?
45. What's your ideal place to live right now?
46. If you won the lottery, what would you do with the money?
47. Are you superstitious? If so, name one. If not, why not?
48. Did you learn to ride a bike as a child? When?

49. Do you have a celebrity crush?
50. Do you enjoy being kissed anywhere unusual?
51. How do you feel about technology?
52. Do you worry about the future of the planet or our species?
53. Do you enjoy live music?
54. How do musicals make you feel?
55. What's your idea of a perfect vacation spot?
56. What advice would you give to 15-year-old you?
57. What's something you can't live without?
58. What is one thing you love about yourself?
59. What is something you wish for?
60. Are you afraid of dying?
61. Have you ever felt lost in grief?
62. Did you enjoy your childhood in general?
63. Have you ever given up on someone and regretted it?
64. Would you pose nude for a live art class?
65. What's the strangest place you've had sex?
66. Did you think you wanted to be a parent when you were a kid?
67. Can you tell me about a time you surprised yourself?
68. Would you describe a sexual fantasy you've had to me?
69. Do you enjoy games or puzzles?
70. Where do you see yourself in five years?
71. What kind of travel do you like most?
72. What's the scariest memory you have?
73. Do you ever wish you could read my mind?
74. Where would you want to spend at least six months before you die?

75. Do you enjoy or want to try a riskier type of activity, like BASE jumping or skydiving?
76. Whom do you admire?
77. What is your idea of the perfect morning ritual?
78. Do you know any lullabies?
79. Are there any sounds or textures that make you shiver or your skin crawl?
80. How does the phrase "life is a journey" sound to you?
81. Do you have a favorite word?
82. What makes you feel better when you are sad?
83. Are you grieving anything right now?
84. Can you tell me about a really joyful moment from the past year?
85. What does it feel like for you to not know the answer to a question someone asks?
86. Do you get curious easily?
87. Have you been bored lately?
88. If you could eat only one food for the next year, what would you choose?
89. What's your favorite kind of celebration?
90. Do you enjoy philosophical questions?
91. Do you like to sleep alone?
92. What is a scent you love?
93. Would you rather lead or follow?
94. Are there stories your family tells about you that you really wish they wouldn't?
95. Do you own anything irreplaceable in sentimental value?
96. What is your favorite way to spend money when all the bills are paid?

97. Would you go back to school if you could? What for?
98. What's the weirdest thing about you that you like?
99. When was the last time you were scared?
100. What is something that you love about me?
101. Do you like clowns or are they scary?
102. What is your idea of a fun summer night?

Key Takeaways

- Entrepreneurial ventures teach us how to tolerate the risky feeling of connecting with others, and we can bring this capacity home.

- You are not just your persona, but you might feel like you are supposed to keep up the masked version of yourself even at home. Get to know who you are beneath society's expectations and share those parts to increase connection and deepen your partnership.

- In our busy life, it is easy to stop being curious about our partner and find ourselves in a rut. Curiosity is the best tool to reawaken interest in who our partner is.

- If we risk being seen, we gain the opportunity to be loved. Have courage!

$$Chapter\ 7$$

Getting What You Need

"Oh, he knows the rules," Erika responded. I asked her to tell me more about the conversations she and Kevin had about their relationship rules. I study jealousy, so I'm fascinated by how people make the agreements about how each of them wants to be treated. Erika's smile froze when I asked her to tell me more. Her brow scrunched up and she said, "Um, you know, I don't think we ever had a real conversation about it. They're just the rules, you know, the rules everyone has: don't flirt, don't text with other women unless I know about it, and be honest with me. It's nothing special he'd have to remember." But the look on her face was troubled. As the conversation unfolded, she realized that she didn't really know what he thought the rules were. And if she was honest, she didn't follow all of those rules herself. She just used her best judgement and trusted herself. Trust is <u>awesome</u>, but trust without explicit communication is an accident waiting to happen.

If I were to choose one skill to be taught to every person, in hopes that we could change the nature of relating, it would be how to make explicit agreements in our personal relationships. Even those who are strategic and explicit in their business life often don't transfer this skill to their love life. What we tend to do is to count on implicit agreements, and routines built on those implicit agreements, to hold up our daily lives. Not sure about this? Consider the roles you carry in your home life. You probably had a discussion at some point about some basic chore distribution when you first started living together, and hopefully you talked about how you would handle your careers if you had children and what that would mean for each of you. As I was interviewing couples for this book, I noticed that most couples have a few of these conversations early on and then hope for the best over the following years. For the most part, it doesn't go too badly, or so it seems if you talk to the two parties at the same time.

Separate them and it quickly becomes apparent that the number of implicit agreements is creating trouble under the surface. The deals built on outdated conversations frequently lead to passive-aggressive attempts to create change without direct communication. The worst part of this situation is that the little annoyances of our lives together can cover up the stuff we really want to change. Most of the time it isn't who takes out the trash or empties the dishwasher that is causing hurt feelings and distance between partners. It's not even just an uneven distribution of chores and responsibilities (though that doesn't help anything). The real source of conflict is all that is going unsaid.

I get it. It is easy to coast along on autopilot, counting on the rhythm of your days to hold everything together. But while you are doing that, each of you is still learning, growing, and changing. You are becoming. This becoming is a double-edged sword. On the other hand, if you engage with your partner and yourself as ever-changing beings, you will never be bored. On the other, those changes require new agreements, check-ins about needs and wants, and lots more conversation. There has to be flexibility in the agreements we make to allow for us each to change. But without making our needs and desires explicit, we won't even have the chance to be flexible. When we rely on the mushy ground of implicit agreements to leave room for each other, we are at risk not only of being hurt, but of hurting each other—all for want of some heartfelt sharing.

Designing Your Relationship

What is your relationship FOR? Most people never really ask themselves this simple question. Even contemplating it can bring a fresh perspective to your life. This question is worth special attention:

What is your relationship for?

If you have an answer right now, please write it down in your journal or in the margins of this book. But honestly, if you feel like this is a silly question because the answer is too obvious to even bother naming, well, you aren't alone! We tend to follow a script when it comes to romantic relationships. We see those around us and a plethora of books, music, and films suggesting that we should marry so that we will feel ooey-gooey in love for ever and ever. And we will feel secure. And we will have a partner in all things. And that person will grow old with us. And we will have a best friend in that person. And we will share financial risks. And we will be each other's family. We will probably aim at children and a home together. The list goes on and on. Maybe those things are true for you—that's totally cool. But even if that describes your relationship's purpose, I have a suggestion I would like you to consider.

What if the purpose of your loving, partnered relationship was to support each other in becoming the best, most unique version of yourselves possible?

This kind of relationship is described by the controversial Jungian theorist Adolf Guggenbuhl-Craig as soteriological. He meant that relationships could be a salvation. In other words, our intimate relationships might be designed specifically to aid each other in the process of individuation—another overly fancy word. Depth psychology is awesome, but the jargon level is ridiculous! Individuation is what Jung named the process of growing more whole and self-aware simultaneously. Individuation is what you were already working toward when you picked up this book. You were seeking more, looking past the habitual, and imagining a deeper, more loving you. You got on the individuation path, even if you didn't know it. Building on the earlier work of Jung, Guggenbuhl-Craig makes an intriguing argument for marriage to be imagined as a container for psychological development.

Put more simply: Relationship can be a spiritual experience if we choose to see it that way.

Warning: This kind of relationship won't be entirely comfortable, and it won't always feel secure. Sometimes it might even feel a bit scary. But the challenge of a soteriological relationship is balanced by a profound purpose: becoming the most you-est you possible, and the same for your partner. That's a pretty sweet payoff. In my experience, this is a relationship worth the investment.

I didn't really understand what it was that I was looking for in a relationship when I got married the first time. I was 20 years old. I wanted someone to wake up next to, and I wanted to believe in them forever. I hoped for comfort and security. That's all fine, but life will have its way with us no matter our wishes. What I never considered was how my dream of security was a childish one. I don't mean everyone's is, but the way I wanted to feel secure was to have things stay safe and the same. But I was a kid. I couldn't imagine how much (or how fast!) I would change. It never occurred to me that hoping for security was a self-limiting pattern.

It came as quite a shock when I finally realized that by trying to stay safe and sound, I was crushing myself inside an outgrown shell. I was 33 and a mother of four children when the pain really set in. When the soul feels constricted beyond tolerance, messy stuff happens. For me, that mess manifested in overwhelming longing for another life altogether and a shocking and sudden desire for someone who was not my husband.

I won't recommend my path to anyone. I threw a grenade into my life. I almost lost everything, even my kids. I actually did lose some of my most treasured friendships and a whole lot of dignity. My life looks entirely different now after a long climb out of that dark pit.

The details aren't as important as the lesson I learned: Choosing my psychological growth was worth the pain. But if I had known that psychological growth, the space and support to be fully myself, was the driving force behind my brutal divorce, I could have probably saved a lot of people a lot of pain.

I wouldn't trade my experience, but I do wish I had known to look deeply inside for the wisdom I needed before I ruined a couple of businesses and a couple of marriages. But we all learn in our own time. My lesson came at a hefty price, but one for which I am willing to claim responsibility. Once I knew what the purpose of relationship was for me, I was able to create exactly the kind of love I always wanted.

The biggest gain? Utter clarity on the purpose of my marriage: We are committed to each other's individual growth above all else. It's not quite what I was told to hope for as a child, but it <u>is</u> satisfying and never, ever boring!

Action Step: Designing Your Unique Relationship

Partnered if possible

The core question of this exercise is: **What's our relationship for?** That can be an overwhelming thing to ask, especially if you've been following the typical cultural script. There's nothing wrong with that, but this single question can turn typical into deeply intentional. You can design your relationship to fulfill the needs each of you has. This is a multipart conversation. I recommend repeating this exercise as your relationship ages. My partner and I do it formally every three years on the anniversary of saying I love you, but the conversation occurs informally as an ongoing thread at this point. It is a normal part of our love story to revisit our shared purpose and our individual needs. Occasionally, we turn up uncomfortable truths about how we've each changed. Sometimes we have to have a real truth and reconciliation meeting. Once, that even needed to be in our therapist's office. But including this thread in the tapestry of our relating means that we both know there is a future we co-create that takes our growth seriously.

You may want to dive straight into the central question, "What is the purpose of our relationship?" But if that feels overwhelming, try exploring these questions to find your purpose:

- What is your idea of our relationship's purpose?

- Do you think all relationships have this purpose or is ours different for some reason?

- How do you feel about the notion of soulmates?

- How important is security for you?

- How important is personal growth for you?

- How important is passion for you?

- Do you feel worried or excited at the thought that we are each growing and changing all the time?

- Do you feel that our relationship plays a role in our spiritual or psychological development?

Remember, these are evolving conversations. Don't spend too much time worrying about having the right answer or even whether you agree about your answers right now. Just entertaining these questions is a phenomenal upgrade to the state of your relationship. It's okay to be unclear or disagree. The point is to consider and start talking about the many things relationships can be for. We are lucky enough to live in a time and place where relationships can be designed to suit our preferences and desires. This has only been true for a few decades, so let's live it up!

Explicit Agreements

Now let's shift back from the grand design of your relationship to the mundane details of it. Every day, you make agreements large and small with your lover. Typically, when we hash out an agreement, we believe that we have been completely clear about what we want and how we want it. But if we were sitting in front of an omniscient objective listener, they could easily point out how much of what we want went unsaid. Most of us were taught that love should happen almost magically. We got messages that the most romantic kind of love is the kind that reads your mind.

It's true! We can read each other's minds; we humans just use language to do it.

The secret formula: Ask plenty of questions.

Maybe that doesn't sound particularly romantic, but it is far more effective than the alternatives. Relying on implicit agreements or believing that our partner is responsible for reading the world the same way we do is a recipe for disaster. It's also SUPER common. Since most of us already have lots of practice at implicit agreements, this exercise is going to help us practice making what we want explicit.

Tool: Explicit Agreements Template

Before you worry about making an agreement together, you need to be clear on what you actually want. Most people socialized to be young women are still taught to push our needs and desires aside for other people. Even if it wasn't directly taught, we grew up in a world that modeled it in millions of images and stories. We were steeped in that, and it left many of us with a fuzzy idea of what it means to <u>know</u> what we need right down to our bones. Start with yourself, then you can bring this into partner work.

Step 1. Get clear on your needs: Name something that you wish were different. It can be a small thing. Maybe you haven't seen your partner without the kids for months, or you really wish you had time to yourself once a week. Perhaps you have a task that you can't stand and really want help with.

Step 2. Practice stating your need or desire in an "I" statement. Use one of these sentence builders to write it down:

I want to _____ when _____.

I need help with _____ when _____.

I would like to hear _____
from _____ when _____.

Examples:

I want to have one hour on the weekend to myself for reading and quiet reflection, totally alone.

I need help with the change in morning schedules so everyone gets out the door on time.

I would like to hear encouraging words from you when I am waiting for the test results.

Step 3. Make clear what you are asking for: encouragement, a specific action, particular words, etc.

Step 4. Refine the request: Add details about when, where, and for how long you would like this to happen. Paint a picture or give them an example. Remember, they don't see the world the way you do. Increase their ability to meet your need by describing how you would like this to go.

Step 5. Gratitude! Thank them for hearing you out and ask for full buy-in. If they can't agree to the need you have, now is the time to brainstorm together how you might get this need met elsewhere or through self-support. Collaboration on the problem-solving bit can feel just as satisfying as having the need met in the relationship. The goal is to be on the same side, working towards the life you both want.

Okay, now you are prepped and ready to put the explicit agreement template to the test in the next action step. You can only get what you truly desire by knowing exactly what you want and asking for it. Be courageous! Your relationship will be better because you will be bringing your deepest desires into the picture. If the first try doesn't go well, don't give up. Many couples have long-practiced habits of implicit agreements and "not rocking the boat." If this is you, the good news is you have even more to gain from boldly asking for what you want.

When You've Already Tried

What if you have been working hard at being explicit for a long time, but you don't feel heard by your partner? The first thing I want you to do is go through this exercise fully. Sometimes we think we are being clear but in fact we are leaving a lot unsaid, especially if the issue has been going on for a long time. Try going through the steps once and check for results.

If you've tried the full exercise and it landed flat, it's time for a new approach. If you've been talking, try writing your partner a letter or changing the scenery for your next attempt. A long walk in a calm setting can do wonders for shifting the energy of the request. If this still isn't working, it is time to engage with a professional mentor, coach, or therapist. We are not taught the skills of relating, so getting a bit of training is a necessary step for many folks. It was for me. Once I learned how to be the loving person I was—out loud—everything changed. And it has in turn changed many of my clients' lives. Your happiness is worth the investment.

Explicit = Actionable

Communication comes in many forms, but when it comes to getting the love you want nothing beats directness. For most of us, that means saying the words out loud. (If writing, signing, or using an assistive communication technology works best for you, use that.)

This action step is about asking for the outcome you want. The more vulnerable you feel doing this, the more likely it is that you've been hoping to have your partner read your mind or pick up on subtle cues. Sure, your cues might not seem subtle to you, but not everyone gets nonverbal signals, innuendo, or double meanings. If you have not felt that your partner is meeting your needs, the first place to check is whether you actually made those needs clear to them.

Action Step: Crafting an Explicit Conversation

Step 1. What is going on in your life that you can't do without your partner's participation? (Examples: You would like help with a household project, you would like to have more satisfying sex with them, you want to travel with your partner more. Name the thing that would make your life feel more joyful but always feels out of your hands.)

Step 2. What, exactly, do you want to happen? Get super specific, really paint a picture. This might not be the exact outcome, but if you could wave a magic wand what would life look like on the other side?

Step 3. Self-check time. Do you actually need your partner to do something about this or could you do it yourself? In other words, is your partner's participation a necessity or is it a want? Wants are great; have them and pursue the request with full energy, but go into a request understanding the difference so that you can be clear about your bottom line if you start a negotiation.

Step 4. <u>Practice</u> the conversation you are going to start. This step is often skipped. In the hopes of protecting our deepest desires from being made too visible, we hint around and avoid saying exactly what we want. By practicing, you'll make that first awkward moment so much easier. The secret method to making this work: **Practice it out loud.** Really. Think about what you want from your partner and say it out loud in private several times. Repeat the words until they have lost that taboo-fear reaction. This step <u>greatly</u> increases your chances of getting it all out there!

Step 5. <u>Action time!</u> Choose wisely to maximize a productive conversation. Choose a time when you have privacy with no distractions. Make sure no one is hungry, angry, lonely, or tired (H.A.L.T. for short) when you start this conversation. Remember that the goal isn't to get exactly what you want but to be able to have a frank conversation about your wants and to negotiate with your partner to find an outcome that works for both of you.

Courage. You can only get what you want by braving the vulnerability.

Including Your Partner in Your Project Relationship Experience

As an entrepreneur, you know that you will face setbacks. Not every idea will sell and some of them will cost you fairly significantly. In those dark times, you have a vision to pull you forward. You don't wallow in every defeat; you evaluate what happened, look for what could be done differently, and make changes. Your optimism keeps the business alive, even when the numbers aren't friendly. That optimism allows you to find what is working in your business and grow it while you let go of what doesn't work. You know that your business requires you to believe in it. If you don't, it will die!

The same holds true for your relationship. Optimism, the belief that things can and will get better, can make all the difference in the world. I don't mean reckless optimism—a childish hope that things will get better without action. I mean that if you apply critical thinking and active participation strategies to the problems of your relationship, and if you invest some strategically planned time and energy on new patterns, it absolutely can get better.

What if They Don't Want to Participate?

There are several reasons why one partner might not want to work on this with you. Maybe they have tried in the past and feel it will be a waste of time. Maybe they are under intense stress and think some other time is a better one to start. Maybe they aren't really in the relationship at all anymore (ouch, sorry, but it might be true). IMPORTANT: Don't jump to any conclusions if your first overtures toward a renewed relationship fall flat. When you picked up this book, you made a choice to work towards a more joyful relationship. With each page you have read, you've reinforced that choice. Your partner might not have been aware there was a problem. The implicit agreements you've been holding up may have cloaked your dissatisfaction well enough to mask the need for a new plan. You have already started implementing rituals of connection to support deeper relating. This sets the stage for tackling the more intense areas of couple-hood in the next few chapters. If there has been resistance from your partner before, try not to lose heart. You have begun asking for what you need in clear, specific language. This is a huge step—one that I see people miss every day and one I missed for years too. You are on a new path now, taking action and creating the relationship you deserve!

Key Takeaways

- Explicit communication is the only way to be sure you and your partner are on the same page. It is far less common than you might think.

- Some people were brought up to think of implicit communication as more polite than explicit. If one or both of you doesn't want to be clear about boundaries, needs, or wants, this part of relationship building might feel "wrong." Try building safer-feeling times to practice sharing and making requests in clear language.

- Practicing explicit communication might feel goofy, but it pays off. Craft your conversation ahead of time and use the explicit agreements template to guide you through the process.

- Set yourself up for success: Make sure neither of you is hungry, angry, lonely, or tired (H.A.L.T.) when you are making explicit agreements. Address those needs first or you might find yourself in an unnecessary fight.

Chapter 8

Sex

You popped open this chapter probably thinking one of two things, either "Who the hell has time for sex?" or "Please, oh please, let her have an idea about how I can get laid tonight." I've been on both sides of this particular problem, and neither is a comfortable spot. Desire mismatch is the most common complaint I hear from coaching clients. If you think about it, this is completely reasonable. Sexual desire is complicated, influenced by myriad factors like hormones, mood, stress responsiveness—not to mention baseline interest in sex as an activity. There is no "correct" amount of sex to have. Some couples agree to a sexless partnership and that is completely fine. The crucial word in the last sentence is "agree." But more often than not, when partners aren't in sync sexually it becomes more and more difficult to talk about sex at all, much less come to a mutual agreement about its frequency. And then, the discord in the bedroom often seeps into the rest of life too.

Abby lowered her head a bit and looked at the floor when she told me that she and Josh hadn't had sex for over two years. "It's just too much work and besides, at this point it would be even more awkward to bring it up." Of course, they were feeling pretty awkward walking past the elephant in the bedroom every day too so, really, what was there to lose by trying something? It turns out, quite a lot. Rocking the boat went against everything Abby understood about love. Being in love meant never making each other uncomfortable. And since they had both been raised with a lot of shame around sex, it came naturally just to never talk about it. But two kids and two businesses later, Abby and Josh were more like roommates than lovers.

But learning how to talk about sex doesn't just happen overnight. Most of us were raised without access to comprehensive sex ed and with plenty of puritanical social values baked into our families, schools, politics, and religions. That is a lot to work through, not to mention the nonsense idea that sex should just happen "naturally." Pfft—no! Sex is something we learn, just like any other activity in life. You weren't born knowing how to expertly craft a media strategy, and it's normal to need to learn how to give and receive sexual pleasure.

Abby had a story about sex that made it hard to even know where to begin, and she didn't know she was writing the story herself. She made a ton of assumptions about what Josh wanted, what he liked and didn't like, and what was totally off limits for them; she was certain they'd tried it all already and there was nothing to do about it now. I asked her what she meant when she said they hadn't had sex in over two years. She looked at me incomprehensibly, "uh...sex, you know. Making love." I pressed her to describe what sex is and after five or so minutes of gentle questions, Abby said, "Crap, do I actually know what sex is? I wonder what Josh thinks sex is?" That was the beginning of a whole new conversation—not just about what sex is for each of them but about how they could co-create a sex life that suited them. There isn't one true definition of proper sex, so you get to decide for yourselves. But first, you have to take the brave step of talking about it.

Disagreements over sex are often a mess because we struggle to communicate exactly what we mean when it comes to sex. What exactly are you requesting when you say, "I want to have sex"? When I ask a room of adult students to write down their definition of sex, I get vastly different answers. Literally no two definitions are the same, even in rooms full of professional sex educators and therapists. Some folks include everything past a peck on the cheek in their definition of sex; others draw the line at some form of penetration. For some people sex starts with feelings, and for others sex feels like an entirely physical instinct. Frequently, once I start reading definitions of sex from around the room out loud, everyone starts scribbling on their own card, adjusting the limitations they hadn't noticed they were placing on themselves just a few minutes earlier. The most important thing isn't to have an exhaustive definition of sex. The most important thing is that we somehow get to a working definition that is shared <u>explicitly</u> with our partner.

Action Step: What Is Sex, Anyway?

Partnered if possible

It's time to put some energy into defining what we mean when we talk about sex. We want to add to our shared definition so that conversations about sex can happen in a meaningful way. To make a meaningful and useful definition, we need to be clear about our context. In other words, a definition that works well in a middle school sex education class will differ from one used in a sex therapist's office. When it comes to sex, context always matters. For this exercise, define sex in a way that suits your life; don't worry about what a legal or medical definition might be. This is personal.

Step 1. Define Sex

- Give yourself a few minutes to think about sex.

- When do you know it has started?

- What act(s) are always present?

- How do you know when sex is over?

- How many people have to be involved for you to consider it sex?

- Does it have to involve pleasure?

- Is penetration required, and if so, by what exactly?

Write a definition that works for you. Don't worry, it is a work in progress, always. My own definition shifts every time I do this exercise too. Getting something written down will allow you to do the next exercise, so please don't skip it.

I strongly suggest making this a team effort. This is one of the most crucial intimacy-building conversations people can have. It doesn't matter if your relationship is six months, six years, or six decades old. This is game-changing, life-altering, reinventing pleasure stuff. Just try it.

Fantastic! Writing down our definition of sex is a powerful first step to acknowledging what we value and desire from our sexual life. Hooray! Let's see if you want to expand your definition now.

Step 2. Refine & Elaborate

Many people find that they don't even have a definition of when sex starts, but instead they identify it afterwards. In other words, did someone have an orgasm? Then it was sex. But focusing too much on an orgasm leaves so much on the table and neglects SO

MANY sexy pleasures to be had even if orgasm is elusive or just not desired right now.

Answer the following for yourself as you feel today. Don't worry about who you were 10 years ago. Stay in the now.

For me, sex starts: _____.

Examples:

- When I hear something enticing

- When I notice my arousal in my body

- When I wake up

- When I see someone I love

- When I am touched in a pleasurable way

- When I am touched in an intimate place

- When I touch myself with sexual intent

- When I feel my orgasm start to build

- When I touch someone else in a pleasurable way

For me, sex has to involve _____.

Examples:

- Consent on my part

- Consent on my partner's part

- Pleasure

- Love

- Physical sensation

- Mental stimulation

- Oral stimulation

- Aural (hearing) stimulation

- Genital sensation

- Naughtiness

- Playfulness

- Toys, costumes, or props

- Penetration

- Fantasies or stories, privately in my mind

- Fantasies or stories spoken to/with a partner

- Pornography viewing

- Intensity

- Gentleness

- Consensual pain

- Ritual

- Sacred intention

- Orgasm

Sexual Fantasies

Now that you know what sex is for you in the physical realm, you can expand your sexual exploration into the realm of your imagination. Your sexual fantasies contain treasures; the imaginal figures you interact with are each important parts of psyche and can be understood as windows into the unconscious—a way to know yourself more deeply and if you are brave, a way to share yourself with your partner.

All sexual fantasy is normal. Fantasy is not equivalent to behavior. This is crucial because sometimes our fantasies are of things we are morally or ethically opposed to in our waking, or conscious, life. This is fine. Think of sexual fantasies as metaphors, much like our dreams. Your mind and soul will use vibrant, even shocking imagery to draw our attention to an aspect of our inner self. If psyche used common, tame imagery it might not be noteworthy enough to create psychological change.

A note on masturbation (solo sex, sex for one, playing with yourself—call it what you like): Sexual energy spent on yourself is healthy and natural. Solo sex is a fantastic way to get to know your own body and provides time for you to explore your fantasy material without the constraints that a partner inevitably adds. Sharing is great, but please do indulge yourself in some private time too—you are worth it! If you have shame come up when you consider touching yourself, I strongly urge you to seek out a qualified sex therapist or educator to help you work through it. The benefits of masturbation are many and there is help out there to guide you through the shame maze.

Action Step: Getting to Know Your Sexual Fantasies Better

If you have had a repetitive sexual dream or a memorable recent one, try working with the dream. Is there a person, figure, animal, or other being in the fantasy? In a quiet space, try to recall as much detail as you can about the other(s) from the dream. Write the dream down. Don't worry about whether you are exact; just focus on putting down what you remember with detail and let whatever needs to come out get onto paper.

Okay, now is the time to play. Set aside a bit of time to enjoy your body. If you have a masturbation practice, great, go ahead and add this to the routine. If you don't, give it a try. Be intentional, get some fantastic lube, take some time for yourself. Enjoy yourself!

To develop your fantasies, you can invite one of the fantasy figures from your dreams or daydreams into an active relation with you while you masturbate. Some of you are thinking, uh...yeah...is there another way to masturbate? But lots of people don't think to interact with their fantasies. If you haven't, give it a try!

Allow the Others in your fantasy to "speak" to you. Go ahead and speak out loud if you are comfortable. Don't feel constrained by the initial fantasy. Instead, let the fantasy figure play with you and allow the fantasy to become whatever it will. The only intention here is to deepen your relationship to the imaginal figure who has already been in your fantasies; often, this figure has a message or a purpose in your life. This action step can be done over and over again. Your imagination is a powerful asset, so take advantage of it!

Action Step: Writing Up the Spice

There is no better erotica for you than what you create in your mind. Yet many of us never tap into the creative reservoir in this way. One idea is to write up a short story. Don't worry about the writing quality; just get your idea of sexy and sultry down on paper or recorded digitally. Alternatively, you can write a letter to yourself as though you were your own dream-lover. Let yourself use all the sexy words you enjoy, and let the Other write whatever they like. Try not to censor them (remember, this is a way to get to know another aspect of yourself). If you are feeling ready, you could share this with your partner, but don't feel like you have to rush to that step. If you are feeling bold but you've struggled with saying things out loud, try writing a story together.

Speaking of Sex

Words have power. Claiming your right to uttering taboo words is a helpful step toward increasing your erotic awareness. When you consciously bring taboo words into the light, you uncover hidden sources of joy, pain, arousal, and excitement. The word "taboo" today means prohibited by society, but the origins of the word are far more interesting. *Taboo*, from ancient Polynesian languages, means sacred, holy, consecrated, and forbidden. Our words have power, and all the more so when certain words are forbidden (even if you are just forbidding them for yourself!).

Everyone has a different set of words that feel illicit to them—words that are hard to say or bring up uncomfortable feelings. The point of this exercise is to become aware of the words we struggle with. In them are clues to what lies in our unconscious. The point is not to make every word comfortable. It's okay if some words make you shiver or just turn you off. There is no shame in having feelings about certain words. It is, however, very useful to consciously know what words are evoking in us. Sometimes you'll have a visceral reaction to a word but then, if you reflect upon it, you'll find that there is something about that word that is also intriguing. Even if some words are totally abhorrent to us, knowing that moves those words a little further from the shadow, and what we can see is far less likely to jump out and spook us!

Action Step: Words for the Mood

Partnered if possible

This exercise is best done with your partner, though doing it on your own can definitely help bring some insight into what words work for you and which ones are total turnoffs, so don't skip it if you can't get buy-in yet. Schedule a bit of time when you can have enough privacy to speak openly in a place you won't be embarrassed to say sexual words.

Read these words out loud and put a check next to any that give you a difficult feeling. Use the somatic check-in tool. Hate a word? Scribble it out! Love one? Put a star or heart next to it! Add other ones that I missed. Add any sexy words that give you a yummy sensation. When you are done, talk about what words you are comfortable with calling your own body now and what words you would like to try out during sexy play but aren't sure about yet. Tell your partner your deal-breaker words.

Vulva	Lick	Munch
Front hole	Pound	Clit
Penis	Going down	Finger
Vagina	Clitoris	Ass
Slit	Dirty	Whore
Dick	Suck	Cock
Cunt	Shaft	Mound
Slut	Pussy	Blow job
Piss	Balls	Cunnilingus

When people do this exercise, they almost always find out that there is a word they've been saying that their partner doesn't really enjoy. MAKE SPACE for change! This is awesome! If you finally give each other the playbook to your erotic language, you'll be one step closer to knowing each other and to knowing you're turning each other on, not off, in the middle of a juicy moment.

Boundaries Revisited: Sexual Intimacy

Intimate relationships need boundaries too, though some of us had a less than ideal model for this in our early life. Opening ourselves sexually to our partner can be a big challenge if we have trouble with boundary setting. After all, if you don't know where your edges are, it can be really easy for your partner to overstep them! Even if you do know what your boundaries are, it can be a challenge to express them inside your most intimate relationship. It doesn't help matters that most of the love stories our culture is soaked in have depressingly conflated boundary breaking with "true love." Gag. Someone who loves you will respect your boundaries. Loving someone does not mean you give them a free pass to do whatever they want to you. It's easy to say that, it sounds perfectly reasonable, and yet boundary disrespect is astonishingly common behavior in partnerships. When it comes to sexual intimacy, developing our communication strategies is critical. The previous exercises get that ball rolling and this one brings physical touch into play to start really working the overlap in physical and emotional boundary setting.

Action Step: Intimate Boundary Exploration

Partnered

You are going to practice saying yes and no in a low-risk context. This comes easily for some and is tough for others. You will need a partner you trust, a blindfold, several food items that neither of you are allergic to—something sweet, something salty, something sour, something a bit messy—and enough time to relax with each other, at least 45 minutes.

Phase 1. Practicing saying yes and no. Sitting comfortably facing each other, the first giver will make a small request for touch—to massage your hand, stroke your cheek, or rest their head in your lap for a few minutes.

The requests can be repeated, and you can give a yes or no at any time. The receiver's job is to say yes to some and no to other requests.

After 5 to 10 requests, switch roles. Go slowly. It is important to let yourself feel the YESes and NOs from both sides.

Phase 2. Now you will deepen this experience. This time, the receiver will put on a blindfold (or close their eyes). The point of removing the visual is to let yourself go deeper into the sensation of saying yes or no. If it pushes your edges, of course, remove the blindfold. The exercise will still be valuable!

The giver will ask the receiver if they may place something in the receiver's mouth. As the receiver, you can practice putting limits on what you are open to receiving or you can choose to be surprised. Try saying a "YES, but...nothing sweet" or "NO, but I would love a kiss." Make your own requests up; just be sure to try out some YESes and some NOs before you switch roles and repeat the process.

Assessment: YES and NO

Partnered

- How did it feel to receive a YES from your partner?

- How did it feel to receive a NO from your partner?

- How did it feel to give a YES to your partner?

- How did it feel to give a NO to your partner?

Action Step: Yes, No, Maybe Lists

Partnered

Have you ever wondered what your partner's more... uh...edgy limits are? Do you have some stuff you'd like to ask about, but you are still feeling shy, even after these exercises? A Yes, No, Maybe list might be just the thing for you and your partner. There are quite a few different kinds. My favorite is an online version like the one at www.mojoupgrade.com because it lets you each see only the things that you both put on the yes or maybe list. You can safely mention you are into something kinky and if they don't also check that item off, then your answer will be left off your joint list. While I encourage you to delve into talking about your sexual desires with all the gusto of a toddler in a candy store, I know it can be both exciting and stressful at the same time. What will they think? Can I really admit this? An online yes, no, maybe can get the conversation started quickly. There are also paper versions; print a couple off, take a couple of pens, and head to the bedroom for a slightly nerdy sexy time. If you checked off yes on this list, I recommend it be one of those full-body YESes we went searching for earlier. Maybes are exactly that—maybe—not a yes or no. Use maybe if you have some reserve but you are open to discussing trying this thing under special circumstances, or maybe you are up for it if they have a strong desire because it feels pretty neutral to you. The key to this activity it to claim your NO with full power. Sex is so much sexier when we feel fully in our power to say no. (Okay, there are kinky situations where it is plenty fun to say no, but that is a negotiated thing and a whole other book. Stella Harris wrote a great one; it's listed in the notes!)

Back to the Basics of Kissing

Once you realize that loving someone means acknowledging their separateness, it gets a bit easier to treat love as a verb. Each of you will feel love in a bunch of different ways and no one can expect to feel perfectly loved all the time. But we can all work on being in better sync with our partners.

One of the little things that can make a difference is finding a way to include more kissing. I know—kissing isn't everyone's idea of a good time, so if it really isn't yours, feel free to skip this section. But first, take a couple of minutes to reflect on why you don't like kissing. I once counted myself among you; I thought kissing was super overrated. I just could not figure out why anyone cared about it. I never thought to really dig into that feeling though, and I missed a big opportunity. I have two important messages for you if you are kiss-ambivalent and kinda wish you cared:

1. Kissing does not come naturally to everyone.

2. Kissing is a learnable skill.

Why do I care about this at all? Because kissing is such an <u>efficient</u> way to reconnect and get out of your head and into your body after a long day. Kissing can be a wonderful way to get back in sync when things are just a bit "off." Kissing isn't the only solution. You are welcome to keep hating on kissing if you want. But if you'd like to reconsider, here are some suggestions for turning bland smooching into luscious, playful love.

Okay, first thing's first: hygiene. If the reason you don't like kissing is due to bad breath or icky teeth, there is nothing to do but address the issue head on. Tell them. Be gentle—shame will only hurt and will not produce results—but tell your partner that an increase in hygiene is what you need to change your intimate connection.

Action Step: Kissing Tune-Up

Partnered

If kissing is your favorite thing in the world, then enjoy this exercise. You might be surprised by what you add to the mix with some playing around. But if kissing is a less than happy piece of your intimacy, break out the breath mints and jump in; you've got some fun homework this weekend!

Step 1. Involve all your senses. Bring yourselves into the present moment by taking five slow deep breaths together while moving into a gentle face-to-face hug. The best way to become a great kisser is to slow down and tune into the feedback your partner is giving you. Much of it will be subtle—little squeezes of the arms, a stroking on your neck, a tightening of their muscles. Kissing is a time when it is not terribly easy to use words, so now you will develop your nonverbal communication. Mashing teeth is a big turn off, so go in slow and gentle, especially if you are reinventing the kiss between the two of you.

Step 2. Playing with pressure. As you start kissing, take turns "leading." Decide who is going first and that person will lean in and offer a kiss with the pressure they prefer. Playing around with how hard and soft you like it is good, but a weak kissing game is often due to pushing the extremes of pressure. Teasing, playful energy is the goal here. Try something new, be willing to break from your current kissing pattern. Take a little risk!

Step 3. Tongue tied. You will add some tongue now, but again take turns leading the kiss, demonstrating what turns you on and then receiving your partner's preferred tongue game. Tongue is the second area where it is common to overdo things. And hey, if tons of tongue is working for you AND your partner, more power to ya! But a teasing, playful tongue is often more welcome than heavy thrusting or fast-moving action, especially when you aren't in the middle of rowdy sex. Try adding some gentle tongue. Everyone is different, but it is safer to ease in rather than try to do too much with the tongue. You aren't performing a dental checkup, so no need to count your partner's teeth.

Step 4. Use that tongue for talking. Share what worked best for you. Kissing is a skill we are expected to just pick up some time during our teen years and never really discuss again. Break that taboo and reinvent your kissing pattern. A whole new world is available if you take the time to create the perfect kiss for the unique couple you are. It is totally okay and normal to have different tastes and to like lots of kinds of kisses in different contexts, but don't forget that mind reading is a poor option for getting what you want. Be bold, be brave, and get the kiss of your dreams by creating it from scratch with your lover.

Fostering Intimacy

Reconnecting is the habit that lets us live our independent dreams while growing together rather than apart. It is the way we can feel secure as truly autonomous individuals without fearing that we will forget each other. Getting in the habit of turning towards one another after a physical or emotional separation makes your relationship resilient. You can trust that even if you have had really differing experiences of the day, you will be able to see each other—REALLY see each other—again. Reconnection is how we stop living on autopilot waiting for the next big vacation to prop up our intimate bond. Don't wait, reconnect regularly and make it a practice. Intimacy thrives on frequent, individualized reconnection.

Reconnection can take many forms, from a kiss and hug hello after a day of working separately to a phone call during someone's commute to a mini-break getaway. The specifics are completely up to you and your partner, but here are two exercises that can get you started with developing your unique reconnection rituals.

This exercise is a deep reconnection, though it is quite simple. It might get a bit woo-woo, so feel free to blame me if your partner is a bit confused about the strange activity, I don't mind!

Action Step: The 30-Minute Deep Date

Partnered

Invite your partner to a 30-minute date at home. Choose a spot in your home where you will have privacy, quiet, and can sit comfortably together. Play some soothing background music (whatever works for both of you). Bring a timer and set it for four minutes. You are going to connect through the windows of the soul, or a gooey ball of highly functioning sight cells—whatever you want to call eyes!

Sit face-to-face in a comfortable way, close enough so your knees are touching. Reach out and hold hands if you can do so comfortably. Starting the timer will signal that you can begin eye gazing.

Eye gazing is just sustained, silent, gentle eye contact. You'll each blink occasionally, but don't close your eyes intentionally. Stay with your partner. Focus on really seeing them and softening your gaze more. Allow your heart to open and be seen by your partner.

When the timer ends, thank your partner for their loving presence. A simple thank you from each of you is enough.

You still have time left in that 30 minutes you set aside.

Over the years, we get used to our partner. We know so much about them it is easy to forget that they are dynamic individuals whose likes and dislikes will evolve.

This game is a chance to stay in the likes and dislikes of today.

Take turns showing each other how you like to be touched. I recommend beginning with how you like to feel your partner caress or touch your arm or hand.

Show your partner and tell them at the same time: "Today, I'd like to feel your hand gliding over the surface of my inner forearm very lightly" or "Today, I'd like to feel both of your hands massaging my hands and fingers."

Get specific and SHOW your partner by demonstrating on them before asking them to touch you this way. When you touch each other, use as much eye contact as possible, building on the eye gazing from earlier.

Switch roles.

Repeat this activity, moving to other body areas: back, feet, legs, chest. Linger a bit over each one. When you are the partner doing the active touching, ask for feedback. "Is this hard enough?" "Does it feel better scratching upwards or downwards?" "Would you like the palm of my hand to touch you too, or just my fingertips?"

If you have time, you could expand this activity into more intimate areas, continuing to show exactly how you like to be touched today. If saying the words "Today, I'd like to have my vulva touched like this" is outside your comfort zone, no worries.

One last note about this activity: Don't be afraid to giggle and laugh together. Some of these words and touches may feel new, so you might feel awkward. You may notice that you have no idea what to expect from a person you thought you knew so well. Laughter can take the edge off of all the awkward. Just remember to laugh with each other rather than at each other; this is vulnerable stuff. Take things one day at a time and allow for change as you practice all of your new habits and skills.

Fanning the Flames by...Scheduling?

I cannot leave this chapter without talking about how to fit sexy, physical intimacy into your wildly busy entrepreneurial life. I know you are likely overwhelmed with the way work can swell to fit every moment. Now that you've established what sex is and gotten in touch, literally, with how you and your partner like to touch and talk to each other, it's time to find some time. Remember when you were dating and half the fun was the anticipation of the night? You'd prep for it, think about it, and when it arrived, you were both primed for a good time. That feeling is within reach.

Remember Abby and Josh? Once they started talking about what sex was, they turned up a super-helpful fact neither one of them had realized. They each thought that the other wanted sex to be spontaneous. The story they were telling themselves was that their partner wanted to be swept away in a fit of passion and nothing less would do. Since the sweeping feeling never showed up, they figured that they weren't interested. But many, many people don't feel spontaneous desire and that is just fine! Scheduling time for intimate connection or even being super clear and scheduling time for a specific sexual act can feel liberating. Rather than waiting for some magical spell to be cast, cast it yourself. Put time for sex on the calendar. Remember that sex is whatever you decide it is, so this doesn't have to look like some prefab love scene.

The biggest thing my clients report getting in the way of finding time is the idea that sex needs to be spontaneous or it just isn't sexy. Ditch that idea and find a time for the two of you to devote to each other. Skipping sex for months not because you don't want it but because you think it has to happen without any planning is <u>far</u> less sexy than scheduling sex.

Action Step: Get It on the Calendar

Partnered

Figure out what kind of sex you are looking for and how to ask for it by completing the action steps in this chapter. Think about what time of day tends to work best for each of you and make a plan for how to be in the same place at the same time (or plan some phone sex!). Spend a bit of time negotiating and get that banging on the calendar.

Key Takeaways

- There is no right or wrong amount of sex to want.

- Most people don't actually know what they mean when they say the word "sex." Create a shared definition with your partner to avoid confusion and misunderstandings.

- Find your preferred sexual vocabulary. It might be awkward at first, but once you know which words are turn-ons and which are turnoffs everyone can relax a little bit.

- Practice setting boundaries, even in the bedroom. Strong, clear, resilient boundaries are an asset to intimacy.

- Try making a Yes, No, Maybe list with your partner to add some new play to your sex life.

- Go ahead and schedule time for sex—whatever sex means for you. Don't let the idea of sweeping everything off the kitchen table because you must ravish each other right now get in the way of actually having sex more often. Get it on your calendar!

Chapter 9

Fighting with Love

Zia was halfway through a project when Tom walked in from his day at the office. As much as she wanted to greet him cheerfully, she also knew that the thoughts she was just writing down would slip away by the time he had finished whatever story he'd walked in with. She tried to get the timing set so this didn't happen, but it also felt like her office door was no match for his exuberance at the end of the day.

Zia intended to talk to Tom about his habit of walking into her office and starting a conversation without noticing what she was already doing, but once it was happening she was boiling with frustration. What a time to try talking calmly. She kept staring at the computer screen, didn't say a word, and continued typing away. When she was done with her thought, or what remained of it once he wandered in, she snapped, "That wasn't awesome. What do you need?" Tom had no idea why she sounded so condescending, so he shot back, "I don't need anything, I was just trying that 'reconnection' stuff you keep asking for. See, I told you it isn't easy to talk to you." This was not the first time they had this conversation. In fact, it was probably the 30th time just this year.

When I was studying human sexuality, I learned that couples each have a unique sexual pattern. Each couple develops the sexual pattern of their particular relationship, and it acts as a template each time they have sex. We do this without ever thinking about it. We have certain words we'll use, positions we tend toward, a set of activities, fantasies, and toys we choose over and over again. While I was learning about long-term relationships, I found the same applied to arguing: We create a pattern and then reenact it over and over again throughout our time together.

Most of the time, I find that people have never actually talked about their sexual pattern; they just follow it instinctively. The sexual pattern we create may be either destructive and unhelpful or it can be productive and support our couple-hood and our individuality. Fighting has a similar quality of patterning. Arguments in a relationship tend to become habits. We have particular ways of arguing and things we argue about that follow a basic template, which may be more or less productive for our overall growth and satisfaction.

I'm not going to tell you that you should stop arguing. Avoidance comes with its own relationship costs, and they are steep. Arguing can be communication if everyone involved is being careful with each other's humanity. In other words, it is crucial that we learn how to argue with grace and avoid dehumanizing each other—always.

The trouble with Zia and Tom is that their pattern isn't just unhelpful, it's actually destructive. Each time they fight this way, it spirals up to a point where the words don't even have much meaning anymore; the tone is doing most of the work. They are locked in a habit that doesn't let them actually see each other. Instead, they toss the same old accusations and retorts back and forth. Though the fight starts after Zia feels interrupted, it is the same fight they have when Tom doesn't want to skip a workout for time together or when they can't agree on whose parent's house to visit for Thanksgiving.

The research of John and Julie Gottman demonstrates that couples can find ways to disagree without driving each other away, but that not all couples come to a healthy habit of arguing naturally. The best news from their research is that satisfying relationships over the long haul depend on being friends with our partners. The reason I say this is the best news is that it isn't magic. Friendship is made of millions of tiny actions that result in a compassionate, warm feeling towards another person. Sounds like a good foundation to me.

The biggest bummer found in the Gottman research is that when we fall into a habit of feeling contempt for our partner, our relationship is in big trouble. Contempt grows best when we don't share ourselves fully, and when we count on old agreements without regard for our partner's changing needs and desires.

So why aren't I telling you to stop arguing altogether? I just don't think it is an achievable goal for lots of folks. I'd rather have you focus on making incremental changes on your side of the equation rather than feel doomed because the two of you can't seem to maintain peace at all times. We'll get to some ideas for how to approach your partner about hostility or repetitive arguments. For now, let's keep the focus where you have complete influence: yourself.

So often we hear media pieces about the ideal partnership being 50/50. Does this really make sense? I always wonder why in the world I would want to imagine myself as half of something rather than a whole 100 percent of me, available and ready to put into everything I do. Ideally, we would all be putting all of ourselves into the vessel of our relationship. Bonus: If I'm 100 percent in, I am always able to take action. This is way more fun than waiting around for someone else to make my life work the way I want.

This doesn't excuse your partner from doing their part. In a relationship, all the adults should be 100 percent in, meaning they should be fully responsible for themselves. Are you showing up 100 percent for yourself and for your partner? That's what you have control over. Stop worrying about what they are doing. You do you.

What would it look like to fight with your partner in a healthy way? Is it possible to be in a soulful, loving relationship and still argue? Yes, absolutely. But there are some tricks to it. Just fighting without care is reckless. Setting aside all arguments in the name of peace at any cost is equally perilous.

Seeing relationships up close, not just as a coach but as a participant, is how I finally knew that there was danger at either end of the fighting spectrum. I came out of a volatile home and I repeated that pattern, fighting loud and long for what I desperately wanted from my partner. He came from a home of what I call "extreme peace," and at first we tried to mimic this model. On paper, it seems the preferable one. But, to my surprise at the time, there are dragons over in those peaceful looking homes too.

When not fighting became the rule, several problems surfaced. Some were manageable—I needed to learn some communication skills and he needed to practice patience with me while I was at it. But neither of us expected the huge challenge of managing the passive-aggressiveness that had been the argument substitute in his home. It had been invisible, so it was much harder for us to notice.

While it might sound upside-down to make an argument <u>for</u> arguing with those we love, ignoring topics we care deeply about causes problems too. It isn't whether we fight or not that determines our relationship satisfaction; it's how we fight that matters. Arguing can even strengthen a relationship if we take seriously that you must learn to fight <u>for</u> your love, not against it. The paradox boils down to this: When we fight against each other, we move further from love; if we can fight for our love with love, it's a whole other story.

Fights are usually cloaked in layers of misunderstanding. We want our needs met, but it is all too easy to think we've stated our needs clearly and reasonably when in fact we don't even know exactly what we want. What is an argument about sex really about? What need doesn't feel met? Describe in vivid detail what it would look, taste, smell, sound, and feel like to have that need met. If you don't have a rich, thick description, is it really reasonable to expect your partner to make it happen?

Zia really wanted Tom to see her work as valuable. She didn't always feel like what she was doing mattered, and when he walked in and started chatting she felt certain that he didn't think her work was important. She wanted to ask for reassurance about her choice to quit her job in corporate project management to start a non-profit, but instead she snapped at him and picked on the first thing she could find to put Tom at a disadvantage. Zia might have asked for the reassurance she needed if she had known it herself, but the familiar track of this fight was much simpler and gave her an instant feeling of "winning." Of course, 20 minutes later she was aware that there are no winners in bickering, but in the moment that part of her was nowhere to be found. And Tom? He might have picked up on the pattern and tried something new, but he really did want to connect and he didn't want to waste any time without her once he got home. In his eyes, Zia was so good at everything. Of course she could chat and type—it was just a social media post she was making after all—she's a pro at that stuff. Breaking open our fighting patterns means getting to know what is under our surface reaction and being willing to see how we are participating in the pattern, even when we think it's the other person's fault.

Learning about ourselves—from our sexual self to our fighting self—is like walking along a spiral path. We come back to the same stuff over and over again but with new perspectives and more experiences to inform our understanding. The philosopher Heraclitus said you can never step in the same river twice, as the water is always flowing. I can't think of a better way to describe getting to know yourself. Your partner is an equally dynamic multiplicity. Stay in the mystery of the two flowing rivers you are and there will never be time for boredom. That doesn't mean you'll never fight though, and that's okay. Let's gather a couple of tools that will help you keep those fights from getting out of control.

Tool: Safe Words for Regular Life

Safe word...given the explosion of talk about kinky sex in the past decade, you've probably heard about safe words. But you don't have to be into anything particularly wild to benefit from introducing a safe word into your relationship. The premise of a safe word in kink is that you have an agreement with your partner that if one of you is feeling your boundaries are being pushed or you feel unsafe in some other way, you say the agreed-upon word and all action stops. The use of a safe word makes it clear to your partner that it is time for a check-in and the situation needs evaluation. In the realm of sex, this word might tell your partner that you are feeling physical pain, emotional distress, or maybe you are just completely overwhelmed. Why establish a safe word and not just yell "STOP!" or "NO!"? In consensual, negotiated, kinky sex there are a few good reasons why you might not want to stop every time someone says no, but that's another conversation.

In the rest of your life, it is true that the words "stop" and "no" should work fine to put a prompt end to a situation. It's simple, you holler "stop," and your partner should respect you enough to stop whatever they are doing. However, there is something very useful to be borrowed from the kinkster's safe word practice. A safe word can also diffuse tension and soften a situation. While a commanding "STOP!" will halt action, it is generally not a conversation starter. Most folks don't feel invited deeper into intimacy when they hear that.

A safe word is designed expressly for the purpose of increasing trust and intimacy. It's simple to start using a safe word.

1. Choose a neutral (preferably funny) word with your partner.*

2. Designate what action will happen when one of you invokes the safe word.

3. Try it out! Be generous in your early attempts to use it. It will probably feel a bit odd and that's okay!

*Or choose an action if you tend to get nonverbal when you are upset. Try a gentle finger snap or a quick, light double-tap on a nearby surface.

When you are first learning how to use a safe word in your relationship it can seem strange, but the benefits are worth it. My partner and I both knew about safe words for years before it occurred to us that we could use this tool to end a destructive pattern we had developed. In the summer of 2013, we were planning our wedding and managing a painful business problem involving a competitor who was using some underhanded moves. With seven kids between us, we also had plenty of home life issues to deal with every day. In retrospect, maybe we should have eloped to cut the stress! But we carried on and I started a really bad habit. Whenever Ken and I were meeting to work on this new business problem (which felt completely out of my control), I would start in with good intentions but frequently change the subject to the kids (problems that felt much more fixable). Of course, this didn't address the very important topic at hand, and it increased the tension in our family. Eventually, Ken noticed that we needed a faster way to get out of the unproductive discussion, so we tried a safe word. Because we chose a word that was funny to both of us and one that was completely out of context, when one of us said it, we could reset the conversation without getting into a secondary battle over who changed the subject or why. Most importantly, we could get back on track together rather than driving each other further away with blame. (I know, you are dying to know, but it probably isn't as funny as we find it: Our word is biscuit.)

Tool: Sillier Than a Safe Word

This is the fastest, quirkiest way I have ever learned to end one of those arguments that just goes on and on, without any productive stuff coming up. You know, the kind of fight where both of you are just poking each other and niggling but not actually having any helpful communication. This little shortcut is for when we find ourselves locked in our nonsense, going round and round and forgetting how much we love each other because in the moment we just. want. to. win.

This trick was passed down to me from an old family friend. It's goofy and it might not suit you, but I would be remiss not to mention it. Caution: This is not for ending arguments about our values, goals, or wrongdoings. That would be gaslighting—intentionally disregarding the reality our partner is experiencing. This is a way to break the logjam of feelings when we aren't really fighting for each other but instead are just poking each other out of habit.

All too often, our fights are really two riled up adults accidentally interacting like they might have when they were small children. There's no point figuring out right and wrong while we are in that state. We'll have to find our executive functioning again to get to the bottom of the real problem, if there even is one. Sometimes we fight because we get carried away, letting stuff snowball way out of proportion. When that happens, the first person to recognize that you aren't fighting for each other, that you are just thwacking away and accomplishing nothing, can do this little thing: Sing a song.

Not just any song, your song. It should be something goofy and easy, and ideally it would remind you of good times. Use whatever works for you. I know someone who breaks into a little verse of "I'm Too Sexy" and another who sings an old ragtime ditty. Personally, if you ever hear my husband comically singing Lyle Lovett's "Keep It in Your Pantry," you'll know that the two of us were just locked in a useless battle.

Like I said, maybe living like you are inside a musical won't work for you, but I can't help but be grateful when I hear my partner remember that we actually like each other and we can stop the madness of destructive arguing. Warning: You have to both be in on this or you'll just seem like you are being insensitive or, worse, gaslighting your beloved. Have an explicit conversation about using this silly—but effective—tool.

Sticky Fights

Extended family, parenting, money, kids, whatever it is, most couples have something that they fight about over and over again. Even happy couples. Even those couples who say they never fight. (Remember, each fighting pattern is unique to the couple; yours might be silent.) Renowned marriage researchers John and Julie Gottman found that virtually all couples have at least one intractable argument. This thing just never goes away. Sometimes it is overwhelming, sometimes it is in the background, but it resurfaces over and over again. If the issue isn't an abusive one—no one is being emotionally blackmailed, or verbally or physically violated—then these issues are best handled as a given: something that can't be overlooked but also something that doesn't necessarily indicate you are unhappy in your relationship.

Still, fighting about the same issue every day, or even once a month, takes its toll on your joy and connection if you don't learn how to fight fair. I won't sugarcoat it. If you grew up with poor relationship models, this is probably going to be tough. Even if you did have good models, you face a big challenge.

160

To gear up for this challenge, we are pulling out two simple, effective tools: affirmations and gratitude. I know you already know these tricks but applying them now, when you are about to dig into a topic that causes pain in your relationship, is like pixie dust—it'll help you fly. Affirmations work extra well if you say them out loud. Choose one or more and use these to bolster your readiness for the next action:

- I am worthy of love.

- I live a loving life.

- I am capable of learning.

- I create moments of love with my thoughts, feelings, and actions.

Gratitude is potent. It's tempting to think we are practicing gratitude sort of in the background, but activating gratitude in a tangible way is so effective I can't overstate the value of it. It's also simple and always available. We are going to use a specific gratitude practice I learned from my favorite improv teacher, Pam Victor.

1. Hold your hands out in front of you, fingers gently balled up.

2. Start naming things you are grateful for, one per finger.

3. Do it out loud.

That's it. Simple. I remember Pam suggesting this method as a great way to start each day. Personally, I use it when I find myself beginning to do a negative spiral about someone else's behavior or impact on my life. It doesn't change what is happening, but it changes my reactive brain super fast.

Side note: This exercise can be used to manage a particular relationship or situation by getting more specific. Rather than choosing the easy things to be grateful for, make all your statements be about what you can be grateful for about the person or situation you are struggling with. You just leveled up!

Practice gratitude and using affirmations before you dig into harder self-awareness work. Kindness to yourself and others supercharges radical change. Now let's tackle those sticky arguments.

Finding Common Ground

When you have an argument that seems intractable, it's a good idea to start by looking within. Sometimes the things we fight for aren't even in alignment with our true desires. Do some digging around before you assume that your position is concrete and unmovable. Do you actually care about this thing or are you fighting because that is your default way to express big feelings?

On the other hand, sometimes we just cannot agree with our partner's position. Maybe they think spending time on long vacations is ridiculous and you feel that as a necessary expenditure (something you are willing to sacrifice other things for). Perhaps you disagree on what kind of schooling your first child should have. Or what if you run a business together and you disagree on the direction it should take.

The truth is you don't have to be in perfect agreement about everything. You are, after all, individuals entitled to your own thoughts and feelings. So long as no one is being harmed, try this exercise to find a way forward.

Action Step: Values to the Rescue

Partnered

Step 1. Name the issue—whatever the fight is about—as each of you sees it, in your own words. Okay, put a pin in that.

Step 2. Now, what <u>can</u> you agree on? What values do you share with each other? These are values, so they might not seem connected to the contentious topic at hand. That's okay. Name at least five values you agree on. For example, you may agree on the necessity for rest, though you disagree on how rest is accomplished. Personal development? Creativity? Justice? Commitment to extended family? Playfulness? Spiritual growth? Learning? Generosity? Honesty? Joy? When talking about a specific argument, you might be stuck because you don't see how your partner is actually in alignment with your shared values at the core, even if the two of you see this specific situation differently. The key here is to list as many places as possible where your values do align.

Step 3. Now see if any of those shared values connect to your argument. Find even one core value that you share concerning the bigger picture.

Step 4. With that common value in mind, begin a collaboration. This isn't just a simple compromise. The ideal isn't necessarily meet me halfway (though you might). Honestly, that often means that instead of one person getting what they want, no one does. Stay focused on the values you share. This is a time to work on your new vision. Let go of the idea that you know the two options available and brainstorm this thing like you would a messy problem at work. No idea is off the table during this phase. Write stuff down.

If your issue is not actually urgently in need of a solution, you might decide to stop fighting about it and let your ideas percolate on the page.

If the issue falls clearly under one person's role (as discussed in the role clarity section), then you could decide to let that person make the call, allowing the structure of your agreement to carry the weight of the decision.

If the issue seems to be stuck after reimagining from a values-based position, at the very least you can seek some professional help with your list of shared values in hand. It might be best to bring in an objective pro to take a look at the situation and help you find the solution just out of sight.

Still Stuck?

When the Gottmans determined that most couples have intractable arguments, they were developing specific techniques for therapeutic intervention with couples. I think those interventions are great, but most of us aren't heading to therapy with our partners every time this pattern resurfaces. So, if sticky arguments are typical, what can we do? I mean, they still aren't fun.

I turn to the theory of psychological complexes when I am trying to make sense of an argument I have over and over again. A complex is like a clump of psychological, emotional energy formed over the course of life. We all get hurt here and there as we grow up, we all have disappointments that feel overwhelming at times. The energy of those collected hurts cluster together in the unconscious. If I get hurt today in a way that reminds me, unconsciously, of a pattern I have seen before I may feel "triggered" or "set off." In that moment, I feel swept off my feet, responding with emotion that seems outsized for the objective reality of what is happening. Often, we recognize a complex after it has had its way with us.

Erika was telling me about how she lost her mind last week just when she and her boyfriend were heading out for a walk. She was upset thinking back over the moment and how it spiraled out of control so fast. One minute she was looking forward to spending some time in the woods with her love and the next she was screaming at Kevin about which leash to use for the dog. "It happened so fast. I don't know why he drives me crazy. Why can't he just remember what leash to use at the park?" But she felt pretty bad about how she handled her frustration. She did want Kevin to care about the details she cared about, but she didn't want to be screaming about leashes or anything else for that matter.

"We were a little late," she continued, "and I was feeling a bit off. But it wasn't really that big of a deal. Bobo doesn't really even care whether he has the long leash or the regular short one. I don't know. I just wanted Kevin to remember." A little more digging turned up the moment when everything changed. Kevin said, "Let's just go." And with a snap, Erika felt the blood rush to her head and the volcano exploded.

In that moment, Erika wasn't a 34-year-old woman with a successful bakery downtown and friends she adores. She was all of a sudden eight years old and her father was towering over her and gruffly telling her to hurry up, "It doesn't matter which shoes you have, let's just go." But it did matter to her. She wanted the shoes up in her room and he didn't care. This was one of a thousand little moments when Erika felt unseen, like her desires didn't matter. The leash might not have mattered in that moment. Bobo really didn't care. But Erika was overwhelmed by a complex in that moment and that did matter. It caused a fight and ruined their walk in the woods, but even more importantly, it left Erika feeling like she really was the "crazy, angry girlfriend" she desperately didn't want to be. Recognizing the complex at work is how Erika figured out what was going on underneath the surface, and that's the first step to making a new pattern.

We all have complexes—they aren't a bad thing—but they are like speedbumps we should be aware of when we are cruising down the road of life. Even though complexes are not easy to work with (I mean, there it is in the name: It's complex!), learning to recognize a psychological complex at work can help you solve a seemingly intractable problem. Once we know the root of our constant arguments, we can change our reactions to them. Arguments that poke us in those tender complexes won't necessarily stop coming up, but with some understanding, we can stop them from wrecking us. Better yet, we can stop ourselves from spiraling into anger, sadness, or destructive coping methods.

Complexes aren't something to be solved. No one "fixes" their complexes. The complex is just a squeaky spot in the floor that we get used to dancing around. You aren't a broken thing in need of a fix. Your complexes are just ways of describing you. On the other hand, your complexes don't feel good. Usually they don't even feel like something you'd want to admit to feeling. Rooted deep in the unconscious, your complexes are capable of kicking your emotional butt and never even lets you in on why.

The reason I'm going to ask you to get familiar with these tricky buggers is that I have never seen a more effective intervention than self-knowledge. A couple of caveats: First, I'm not blaming your mother or father. Yes, your early childhood has a lasting impact, but we all get bumped about a bit by life. Most parents mean well and they leave fingerprints on us despite their best efforts. If you were in an abusive or addiction-riddled household, then you probably have even bigger scars and they probably feel pretty damn unavoidable. I don't blame you if you are angry about it. And we still need to deal with what you do now.

Do any of these phrases sound familiar?

- I can't believe you.

- You're exactly like my (ex/father/boss/etc.).

- You need to change (this feature of yourself—not an action but an essential part of yourself) if you want me to be (available/loving/nice/aroused/etc.).

- I told you that wouldn't work, now you've ruined everything.

These kinds of phrases shift all the responsibility for the situation onto your partner. They might feel satisfying to say, for about a second. But blaming your partner, even if they did something unfortunate, just drives them away. Even more critical, when you blame you give away your power. You are responsible for yourself and your actions. If the relationship is no longer a good experience for you, then you absolutely may end it. But if you are hearing yourself pushing all the responsibility away, do yourself a favor and double-check what's going on. Whether you break up or not, this is valuable growth material!

Action Step: Name the Complexes under Your Sticky Fights

Step 1. Notice. Where are you repeating an argument? What can you not seem to move past? Do you have an argument where you regularly find yourself thinking, "What the hell am I doing? This isn't like me!" In particular, look for the fights that never seem to resolve despite how regularly the issue comes up.

Step 2. Name YOUR ROLE in the argument; do not name your partner's role (that is for another exploration). This is personal. The complex has an archetypal core, which is just fancy talk meaning that complexes have a universal quality. Our fights revolve around themes that come up for humans all over the world, but the way it appears in your life is totally individual. You've been impacted by a family system and social privileges and/or injustices, and the role you play out will have a lot to do with how all these systems worked on you. Couples tend to find sex, money, religion, parenting, and business to be particularly full of repetitive potential. Are you playing out a child-like role in a recurring fight about money? Do you have a god complex about sex, feeling overly puffed up and controlling in this area? Maybe you argue most often about extended family, and underneath all that you know that you have an unresolved problem with the authority your mother represents.

Remember, what we name we can tame. A tame complex is one that we can dance with, and when it comes to sticky issues in our relationships learning to dance can be the difference between lasting love and fractured fairy tale. If you want to dig into your personal complexes further, check out the additional material found in the bonus chapter of this book.

Key Takeaways

- Couples tend to have fighting patterns that we play out unconsciously.

- Learning to fight with respect means fighting for our love instead of against each other.

- Having a sticky fight isn't the measure of your relationship. Respecting each other, even during fights, means learning how to fight fair.

- Resentment and condescending talk are the fighting warning signs. Establish a safe word to stop the argument from heading down this path.

- It's normal to have some fights that come up over and over again. We can change this pattern by recognizing the underlying pain that keeps leading us down the same track and committing to working through that pain with a therapist, counselor, or friend.

Chapter 10

Talking Business with Love

Business talk is so <u>yeasty</u>. Without attention, business talk can puff up and fill every moment of your life, squeezing out all the other interesting topics you and your partner care about. That can go on just fine for a while, but eventually problems tend to pop up if business talk is the focus of all of your conversations. This happens with even greater frequency if you and your partner each own a business or if you work in the same business. Being "copreneurs" means both of you have an active role in at least one shared business. Copreneurship comes with its own set of challenges and rewards, but even if your partner doesn't work with you it is quite likely that they get to spend a fair amount of time hearing you talk about it.

Sharing our thoughts and feelings about what is going on in our business is natural. Your work matters to you a lot or you would not do what it takes to be an entrepreneur. Talking about the ups and downs of your market, the new strategy you are psyched to try out, or the big hit you just took and how you are going to roll with it are ways of relating to your partner. You are sharing what matters to you. That's great! On the other hand, the entrepreneurial life isn't for everyone and if your partner is the kind of person who loves working for someone else, climbing the corporate ladder, or is a full-time parent they might not get why you are always talking about your business. And that's fair—you get to make your life choices and they get to make theirs. But all the fairmindedness in the world doesn't help when we are out of sync and feeling unseen. Want to keep your non-entrepreneurial partner interested in what you are doing? It's going to take a bit of planning. That's okay, you rock at planning!

Two Magic Ingredients

For some couples, talking about business is the easiest part of their communication, while for others it is one of the toughest. In all of my interviews and coaching sessions, the one thing that has been made most clear is that there is no one template that works for every couple. Instead, the happiest couples worked on two things: clarity and flexibility. Clarity means they take the time to know what they need and want and to listen to what works for their partner. Flexibility means they steer clear of dogmatic rules and instead create a system that works for both of them.

The Non-entrepreneurial Partner

What about those of us who are married to truly non-entrepreneurial types? My husband is an awesome fit for me personality-wise. We enjoy each other's company even on our worst days. But he is not entrepreneurial. I learned this while running a business with him for the first five years of our relationship. That business eventually closed, in part because he really, really does not enjoy the business of being in business. But neither of us knew that when we started dating. Entrepreneurial energy is contagious. He definitely fed off my excitement in those first couple of years. But as the daily grind of finding clients, building systems, and running the operation set in, he was more and more miserable. On top of that, the business formed the center of our conversations. There wasn't enough room left for the us he really wanted. Sadly, it took years for the reality of the situation to become clear to us both. One day after I had been monologizing for an hour about how we could shift the business model to increase our profit margin, I looked over at him and saw the truth: He hated this. His usual sparkly eyes were glazed over and he seemed lost in the millions of options I was lobbing at him. I thought we were having fun, but in that moment it was clear that only one of us was enjoying the moment. I asked him a crucial question, "Do you want to be an entrepreneur?" and with that the spell was broken. He said, "No. No, I don't think I do. I'm not sure I ever did, really." We announced our gym was closing the next day. I do not consider this a failure. In fact, I think it was one of the pivotal moments in our relationship. Rather than seeing and saying what we wished were true, we looked into ourselves and said what was real. Even though it was painful to end something I loved, I didn't want to run the place on my own and I was ready to try something new.

The big win in that experience (aside from the amazing clients whom I adored beyond measure!) was that Ken and I learned that we want very different things from our work lives. We found out that while we loved working together every day, we really didn't love having our business filter into every single moment of our relationship. As we transitioned from that life to this one, we worked to create better habits around work talk. Bringing awareness to our differences made it possible for him to be working at his desk five feet from me all day every day without repeating the misery of our copreneur experience. There is no one rule about how to handle business talk. The key is to bring attention to what works for each of you and create conscious habits that serve the relationship.

Let's Get Talking

When I say business talk, I mean all the conversations about business: mundane details, big financial stuff, employee issues, your hopes and your worries—all of it. Of course it can expand to fill every minute; it's important and you care about it. With that said, bringing conscious intention to when, where, and how you talk business can be a relationship saver.

Right, to the nitty-gritty then.

Assessment: Current Business Talk Habits

- When was the last time you talked about your business with your partner?

- Was that a spontaneous talk or a planned meeting?

- Do you have any time set aside in your day, week, or month specifically to talk business with your partner?

- Where do we talk about business?

- Does your partner have a say in your business?

- How does your partner react to business talk? What is their interest level?

There isn't a right or wrong way to handle business talk. There is, however, a potential danger in not being conscious about it. When work fills up every moment of your life, your partner may justifiably feel left out and unseen. On the other hand, if you never share details of your business, your partner may also feel excluded or confused about who you are. Owning a business isn't just a job, it is a lifestyle. There is always something that could be done. Finding a way to have a life in that lifestyle can be tricky!

Shift Your Context

When work conversations always happen the same way and seem to keep causing the same rifts between the two of you, it's time to make a change. The simplest way to shift energy is to change the context of the conversation. Successful businesswoman and sex educator Marie-Claire Thauvette and her husband run a fast-growing French language school in Canada. When things are going well and growth is the name of the game, you'd think everything would be rosy. Yet, growth also puts a strain on everyone involved (the kind of strain we want, but still!). Always dedicated to making her relationship blissful, Marie-Claire found that moving some of their business meetings from their offices to the forest worked like magic. So, for a weekly meeting, they go for a walk in the woods nearby. The combination of moving their bodies and being in a natural setting relaxes them, allowing for new perspectives and reconnection even if the topic is difficult. A change in scenery can reinspire positivity in a business conversation and even spark fresh ideas for ongoing challenges.

Scheduled or Organic?

Do you feel better with scheduled time for sharing the details of business, or do you like to let it flow throughout your day? I've seen happy, successful relationships handle this both ways. For some, a daily meeting at a set time provides the structure they need to close the door on business issues outside of that time. For others, sharing the details of business in real time without a schedule feels natural and helps them feel connected through all the ups and downs. The important thing is to get clear about what works for you and to check in with your partner to be sure it works for them.

There is a middle path as well. Perhaps you feel best sharing all the time, but you find that you need to carve out some boundaries for specific activities, like business (or sex!). Maybe it's dinner time, breakfast, or the bed and bath time routine with your kids that needs a bit of non-business boundary setting. This is a great place to use the safe word you established in the section on arguments. Remember, the purpose of the safe word is to help your partner quickly see that you feel a boundary has been crossed. It isn't an accusation; it's a nudge back into connection. If the two of you slip into business talk at a time set aside for non-business activities, say the word. Then just shift the conversation back. No blame, no apologies needed. The safe word does its job best when you let it be a gentle reminder to make eye contact, smile, hug, or hold hands. If you are worried that the business idea you had just started talking about is going to slip away, make a note of it the quickest way possible. I generally send a text to my partner or to myself so that it will come up as unread at a better time. The key is to do it fast and return to the moment at hand.

Action Step: Creating Great Business Talk Habits

Partnered

What are our patterns now? Do they include scheduled business meetings, organic flow of business talk, a middle way?

Where do we talk about business? If it feels like everywhere, where don't we talk about business?

Where do we have most of our difficult talks?

What time of day tends to be the easiest for us to talk business in a connected way?

Do we have a safe word to remind us to table a business conversation during non-business times?

Key Takeaways

- Business talk can fill up every moment of our down time, especially if both partners work in a shared business.

- Try shifting the context of some of your business meetings. Try taking a walking meeting or a cafe meeting to change up the energy.

- Work together to figure out what kind of business talk pattern suits you: scheduled, organic, or a blend. The important thing is to be conscious about when, where, and how you talk business with your partner.

- Allow for differences between you and your partner. Not everyone shares our passion to build a company. If your partner isn't the entrepreneurial type, don't force-fit each other into roles that don't suit. Be willing to say the awkward stuff so you don't waste years or decades living a life that only works for one of you.

Chapter 11

Talking Money with Love

Even if you don't share ownership of a business, money is one of the most difficult topics for couples. One study found that fights about money were the best predictor of future divorce. Ack! Most of our money-related relationship trouble lies in a fundamental misunderstanding. When we fight about money, it's not just about money. Money is symbolic as well as practical. Money brings us face-to-face with our biggest dreams and our deepest fears. When money is a source of strife, what's really being fought about are transparency, autonomy, freedom, and security. Under the surface of money disagreements, we are wondering: Can I trust you? Do you value (love) me as I am?

Deep exhale. That's some heavy stuff and it's not like we can avoid the topic. Money is an unavoidable reality for all of us. Owning a business means we feel deeply connected to the profit and loss sheet. Maybe on our worst day, we even measure our worth with dollar signs.

Money is an archetypal thing. It is easily overwhelming in even the most benign-seeming contexts. It carries a ton of taboo as well. Some people feel comfortable talking about money, but far more of us learned to avoid money discussions at all costs. Then, of course, many of us have a money complex to boot. Complexes are basically tons of psychological energy swirling around a particular topic like money or sex. A complex begins when we can't manage the intensity or complexity of something, especially early in life. We get all twisted up and easily confused when we are in the grips of a complex. Even if nothing horrible happens around money, it has so much social and personal meaning that we can find ourselves a total mess in the money arena really easily. As I described earlier, complexes don't go away just because we are safe now. A money complex doesn't just disappear once we've got "enough." They are a part of us, and we learn to dance with them over time.

I have a money complex. Growing up, we always, always, had food on the table and packed into the cupboards. I was warm, dry, and clothed. I got an (okay) education and had plenty of interesting hobbies thanks to my parents' deep creative streak. There was also a lot of fighting about money. A lot. As I grew up, I eventually realized that my parents never really figured out how to deal with money with transparency, so it came up in heated moments attached to feelings of fear and anger. My mom struggled with bipolar tendencies and spent money in a manic frenzy; my dad hated to handle the bills, so he let this happen over and over again without stepping in or offering help. Put a developing psyche (i.e., a child) into that mix and you've got yourself a spicy money complex; by complex I mean a mess of psychological energy swirling around a particular aspect of typical human life. My money complex was born in the peculiar situation of my childhood, but everyone's experience, even two siblings raised in the same household, will be unique. Your money story is yours, just like your interpretation of an abstract painting is yours alone.

My fear around money has never totally left, no matter how secure or safe I've been. The key to handling my own money well began with understanding that my feelings about money are only tangentially related to the objective reality of my fiscal situation. Those feelings are yucky sometimes (a lot of the time), but naming the complex and owning that part of me helped me to finally relax and enjoy the project of money. It's done my business a ton of good, and even better, naming my money complex has given me a way to discuss my irrational reactions with my husband without blaming him or shaming myself. Money still makes my insides swirl and sometimes I get reactive about it. But now I can go with that flow, knowing that if my money complex is active, I should take a break, re-center myself, and get the outside help I need to make great decisions. My husband can use his strengths to meet this complex with love rather than confusion.

If you have a money complex (and so many of us do), learning how to recognize it in action can save you a lot of pain. The next assessment will help you notice how you react to money issues and give you tools to design a strategy for managing the reactive brain that takes over when your complex is driving the action.

Assessment: Money Stories

Both partners, independently

Money causes enough trouble for enough people to warrant a deeper look at what is under the surface.

- What did your parents or caregivers model for you about money? Was it an easeful topic, was it totally off limits, were there fights or fears lurking everywhere money was concerned?

- In three feeling words, what is your relationship to money:_____, _____, _____.

- Money represents_____ to me.

Money has an archetypal quality, which means it tends to take on a sort of god-like or mythical position in our psyche. Do you have any myths or fairy tales that come to mind when you think about money? I know this seems like a strange question, but money is often woven into our unconscious and stories can provide a way to discern what we don't recognize consciously. For example, I resonate deeply with the story of *The Elves*

and the Shoemaker when I think of money. As a child, I
tied money directly to the process of making things and
being an artisan, but I also always expected to need
magical intervention to be fairly compensated. Realizing
this helped me learn to flow with my money complex—
no need to await elves once I realized how I was limiting
my potential through lack of confidence in my work. The
stories that resonate may carry clues about how money
works in your life.

- My money myth/story is: _____
  _____.

- When I am stressed, I tend toward which end of
  the miser/spender spectrum?

- What do I wish I did differently with money?

- Do I keep secrets around money, like secret bank
  accounts, limiting my partner's knowledge of my
  finances, or spending in secret ways?

What we name, we can tame. Working with these
unconscious patterns is a typical part of my coaching,
and always proves surprisingly powerful. When it comes
to love, money talk can be a disaster so hauling this
stuff into consciousness is especially worthwhile. Many
couples may have had a define-the-relationship talk but
totally skipped any mention of define-the-dollars talk.
It's never too late to deepen our connection by opening
up this area of ourselves to each other.

Prep yourself for the action steps by recalling your strengths. What are the key entrepreneurial strengths you identified in yourself in Chapter 2? These serve you well in business, and they will serve you well in your money conversations too. All too often I see well-established, confident entrepreneurs simply nailing their business money goals but completely losing that confidence once they open their joint checking accounts. Remember your whole self; you've got this. And, if money is a struggle in business too, this is a huge opportunity. Figuring out what your money complex is and what money stories you've been living can be the wake-up call you need to get money working for you instead of ruling you through fear.

Action Step: Money Talks

Partnered

Step 1. Set yourselves up for success: Check for signs of H.A.L.T. before you tackle a money conversation. Are either of you hungry, angry, lonely, or tired? Address those basic needs first.

Step 2. Make time for a 90-minute talk without interruption, get a babysitter or use that precious naptime spot, put away your phones, and bring your notes from the assessment.

Step 3. Money talk might be loaded with built-up feelings, so start by taking five slow, deep breaths together. Lean into the discomfort of this discussion; at the very least, you will be one talk closer to your financial dreams!

Tool: Active Listening

Review this tool together before beginning your Money Talk

Active listening means when it is your turn to listen you will focus on your partner's words and body language, stay tuned into them, set aside judgements, nod and use supportive, short introjections like "mmhhhmm" and "I hear that." Reflect what you hear by mirroring back to them along the way and allowing them to correct anything that was misunderstood. Ask questions that deepen the discussion but keep the focus on your partner's story rather than jumping to compare or connect it to yours (that's coming, don't worry!).

Now, it's time to start the money talks.

Step 1. Take 10 minutes each (use a timer) and share the answers to the money stories assessment questions. Allow yourself to be immersed in your partner's money story as if this is the first time you are hearing any of it. When the 10 minutes are up, swap roles and go for another 10 minutes.

Step 2. How do your money stories fit together and how do they seem to clash? Do any of the stories shared make it a little clearer why your partner feels the way they do about money? Give yourselves 20 minutes to really explore how your core money stories have caused misunderstandings or perhaps even a complete avoidance of money discussions.

Step 3. Now it is time for a collaborative vision session. Give yourselves at least 30 minutes for this part. Have some paper handy and write down what you discover together.

- What are your hopes and dreams? Money is inextricably linked to our vision for our businesses as well as our marriages.

- What do you want to accomplish when it comes to money?

- How much money do you want in your savings and investment accounts?

- Do you want to reclaim more time and are you willing to make a financial change in order to make that happen?

- What experiences do you want to have, and how will money make those possible?

This part of the money talk may expose more divergence in your partnership. If one of you dreams of working only six months of the year and traveling the world, and the other has high hopes of putting six figures into your investment account as fast as possible there is a pretty big vision gap to address! When it comes to money, finding a vision that feels great to both of you might take some time. If you find you are really far apart, now is a good time to find a coach who understands the psychological impact of financial couple-hood. When we get married, move in together, or combine finances in some other way, we tie ourselves to another person's money history, money complexes, and money realities. Since money fights are a reliable predictor of divorce, investing time in working through this is highly valuable!

Step 4. Okay, there's no easy way to do this step and not everyone will need to, but if you have been keeping money secrets now is the time to come clean. Money secrets can be just as harmful to relationships as sexual infidelity, and it is tempting to keep putting off telling your partner if you have been less than honest and forthcoming about financial stuff. Some common secrets include secret bank accounts, secret loans or credit cards, secretive shopping, and secret gambling.

When it comes to sharing money information though, don't mistake the importance of transparency to mean that you have to share every detail about spending or even account balances. If having a yours, mine, and ours financial arrangement is what you enjoy, go for it.

The secrecy behaviors I'm talking about are intentional hiding and lying, not an agreement to keep some aspects of your financial lives private. Privacy and secrecy are entirely different concepts. Controlling is another way that money troubles can arise, so if there is disagreement about privacy or other controlling behaviors now is the time to find a therapist or coach to help you address any potentially harmful or abusive trends. When it comes to getting help in this area, the sooner the better.

Step 5. Today you talked about the big themes around money, and next you'll need to dig into the details. Gathering account details, budgeting, and strategic planning are activities that need attention on the regular. To tackle adding money talk to your relational life, schedule regular money meetings now. Grab your phones and get it on your calendars as a recurring meeting. Financial professionals recommend weekly check-ins to keep you both on the same page. I have seen monthly meetings work, but the more frequent the check-ins, the more you normalize talking about this tricky topic. You can also make much quicker course corrections when you meet frequently. Personally, I handle the money in my household and I meet with my husband weekly for 15 minutes right after I pay bills and check our investments. Once a quarter, we talk about visions and dreams, make adjustments, and strategize for the next quarter. We set savings goals and check in to see how we've actually done and ask for support if either of us is struggling with a sticky feeling around money. Normalizing money talk has helped us both find a comfortable pattern around a sensitive issue where we have vastly different histories. When I start to think we can "just skip this one meeting," I know I'm falling into old habits of avoiding money talk. That means it is more crucial than ever and I lean into the struggle.

Key Takeaways

- Money isn't just money; it has a symbolic quality. Money is tied to our sense of self-worth, our biggest dreams, and our deepest fears.

- Be curious about tension around money. What else is going on when we are arguing or avoiding arguing about money?

- Consider how money was handled in your family and how the differences in you and your partner's history with money might be impacting your ability to talk about money today.

- Sharing our money stories with our partner is a critical ingredient in coming to understand why money causes so much confusion. Get to know what money means to each of you.

- Having a big money talk is a guard against divorce and painful secrets. Sharing your money stories, visions, and dreams gets you on the road to a financially healthy relationship.

- Schedule weekly money check-ins to stay on the same page and quarterly vision meetings to keep you both moving towards your goals and dreams.

Chapter 12

When Things Fall Apart

Things are going to veer off course. You are going to lose people, relationships will end, businesses will close or be sold. Change is the only thing we can really count on. Often when people are talking about a breakup, divorce, or shuttering a business, they use the word "fail." Words have power. The way we talk about something frames the emotions we will connect to the circumstances in which we find ourselves.

When things end, especially in marriage and business, our culture encourages the use of the word failure.

My business failed.

My marriage failed.

I failed.

We hear these phrases all the time. I hear coaching clients enumerate their failures a lot, especially when we get past the surface stuff and they show me what they were afraid to admit.

I don't mind if you use the word fail. If it works fine for you, okay. But is it accurate? Is it true that a business is a failure if you close it? Is it true that divorce means your marriage was a failure?

No. Absolutely not.

First, you can't define something as a failure without measuring it in many dimensions. Everything can be viewed from multiple perspectives. Failure is a word that flattens things out. Failure takes all the lessons learned, all the almosts, all the particularities, and tosses them to the side and says, "Hey, you didn't measure up in this one way, so you failed." Yeah, and failure makes it personal. It's not just that the business or marriage failed, but you are a failure.

No. Just no.

I wasted so much time in the trickery of the word failure. When I closed my first business, my only measure of success was whether the doors were open. I forgot that I had made so many people happy through my design work. I ignored how much money I had made over the years, adding to my family income when we needed it most. I set aside how much my skills developed and what I learned about marketing fashion in a small town. Why? Because our society likes to keep things simple. Success is measured very narrowly.

It wasn't until I was signing my divorce papers (along with the documents splitting our various business interests) that I realized that endings really are NOT the same as failures. I felt the pressure to use those words, "failed marriage." But the thing is, they just don't make sense. We were married. We made a family. We grew, learned, changed, and loved. Why in the world would those things not count for more than longevity?

I'll make this simple: My little brother died way too young. He was 36 with three young children and everything to live for when cancer took him fast. His life was in no way a failure because it ended before any of us had planned or expected. That's easy enough to see. The love and learning along the way amounted to nothing short of a miracle—and so are all of our weird, individual adventures. Endings are endings, not failures. Repeat that. When you forget, come back and read this again. The love you made is never a failure. The learning you did is valuable. The end does not define the situation.

Discernment (the good kind of judgement!)

The actual ending of something is often less painful than the prolonged process of choosing to end it. You've been there: You aren't happy at a job, but you're scared that if you strike out on your own, it won't work. You are living with someone you like well enough and maybe it's time to do the next thing, but argh! There are positives and negatives to every option and the process of deciding is eating up your life. Maybe you are in a situation that is comfortable enough (sort of, so long as you ignore your ever-deadening soul), but choosing to move forward means ending something that was once precious to you and so you just stay in the not-deciding place, doing nothing.

For some of us, deciding is so painful we rush it, choosing with reckless abandon. For others, choosing grinds every gear to a halt. Hitting the sweet spot more often is easier if you have some tools for deciding. Luckily, there are lots of them, more than you need. I suggest trying a few new options and settling on a couple that you can use regularly until they are so natural for you that decision-making becomes something you enjoy.

First, I am assuming that you already use some basic tools for rational decision-making. You make business decisions in consultation with mentors and professionals, right? When you are in over your head with the implications of taking on a second location or shifting from an in-person to online business model, you should definitely tap into the knowledge of an expert who can tell you from experience what the ramifications of your options will be. But the choice is still yours. It's the same when it comes to love and relationships. You can and should seek some help, in the form of this book, a coach, a therapist, or a close friend, but only you have the authority to make the choice. Love isn't just about the fuzzy, hard-to-describe feeling. There are practical concerns to consider. But once you've done that, how do you ask ALL of yourself to weigh in on your choice?

It's a bit tricky because part of you is unconscious and therefore isn't available to your rational conscious self. But without getting input from your unconscious, you are leaving a whole lot of your innate intelligence out of the equation.

Being a rational-thinking-type woman, I struggled with this. I mean I really wrestled with it. The idea that I did not have direct access to my entire self made me furious! Yet I was not always rational. I made choices I regretted, spent time doing things that made no sense to me, and let myself get carried away by forces unseen. In other words, I was a pretty typical person. Learning to accept that my unconscious self had significant effects on my life allowed me to come to grips with the reality that my conscious "I" was not the only thing running the show. Reading a lot of Jung led me to begin to diversify the ways I know things. Rather than relying solely on thinking, I gathered several methods for knowing what is under the surface. I didn't trade in my thinking cap for them; these tools are best used right alongside your day-to-day cognition skills.

Tool: Dreams

Writing down your dreams is an investment in your self-knowledge. The unconscious has limited ways of getting through to you during the day when you are busy with mundane tasks and abstract thinking. But at night, you are fair game for your unconscious to present images rich with meaning. Dreams often seem weird. I mean, why would I dream of a snake driving my car?! But the unconscious has only one language: image. This doesn't just mean pictures; dream images can be tonal, verbal, musical, colorful, abstract, or sensational. The unconscious will try whatever it can to present the messages it wants you to receive. So yeah, dreams might seem weird because they are symbolic rather than literal. The snake of my dreams isn't a message to warn me that a literal garden snake is going to try to carjack me.

Some people find that dreams don't appear useful to them because when they turn to dream dictionaries, the meanings listed don't make any more sense than the dream itself. I definitely had this trouble. The turning point for me came when I learned to look for meaning from myself first. I stopped looking for someone else to tell me what the dream meant and began working with the dream image just the way it appeared. I started simply and I would recommend this method to anyone, no special skills required.

Write down your dreams. If you have trouble remembering them, set yourself up for success by putting a pencil and paper by your bedside (I like a little lighted pen so I can write in the dark). Before bed, say to yourself out loud: I'm open to my dreams and I will remember a dream tonight.

Crucial step: When you wake, grab the pencil and paper before you do ANYTHING else. Write whatever comes, even if it doesn't make sense. Don't worry about capturing every detail or writing three pages. Just write down your strongest impressions. Any people, animals, places, or things you recognize? Were there words or feelings? Did you have a strong sensation? Were you watching the dream or in it? I used to get bogged down by my dreams because they were so elaborate that I didn't want to have to write them down. I didn't have an hour in the morning to explain the vivid detail of these odd scenes. I decided that less was better than nothing and it changed my dream experience. Now I write down my dreams in broad strokes, making a quick synopsis, trying to capture the impression the dream left and any stand-out dream figures or happenings. This was the best I could possibly have done as a hyper-busy woman. Since that day, I've collected a stream of unconscious material without investing time I simply didn't have.

Now, play with your dreams. This topic fills up hundreds of books; perhaps you've even cracked a couple at some point. Personally, I found the sheer volume of it all overwhelming. I boiled down my approach very succinctly to one simple idea that works for me and has worked for my clients: Treat your dream figures as if they were friendly messengers. Why? Because those visitors in your dream, they are all pieces of you. If you find yourself afraid of a figure, remember it is a part of you. If you are inspired by a figure, well, that's part of you too. Often, we hold our dreams as if they are separate from us or happening to us when they are actually an integral part of us. You are not just one thing: You are a multiplicity! By befriending your dream figures, you are befriending parts of yourself. I bet you see where I'm going now. By reclaiming more of yourself you will feel more whole; you can empower yourself by simply being all of you. Just like working with our projections, claiming our dream figures lets us be complicated and whole rather than simplified, palatable versions of ourselves.

If you want to work with your dreams further, I strongly recommend the audiobook by Clarissa Pinkola Estes: *The Beginner's Guide to Dream Interpretation*. Most known for her seminal book *Women Who Run with the Wolves*, Jungian analyst Pinkola Estes breaks down the classical form of Jungian dream work, making it very straightforward for anyone who has a bit of time and some dreams they want to work on.

Tool: Somatic Awareness for Discernment

Early on, I had you do a somatic check-in. The shift from taking information in from the outer world to noticing the subtle information from your body is a powerful thing. Applying this tool to the discernment process doubles down on that power. Once you open to this type of knowing, you have a resource always at the ready for double-checking your actions. Are you in alignment with your intuition? Tune into your body. Often, we overlook even bold physical clues like disruptive headaches or digestive issues when we are dealing with challenging decisions, but there are less obvious indicators as well. To access this level of awareness, it helps to do something to short-circuit your conscious brain for a moment—just long enough to get your unconscious self to weigh in.

One simple tool to increase your connection to your inner truth is muscle testing. This is another one of those sounds-kooky-but-give-it-a-try things. I mean, I wouldn't suggest that you use muscle testing in place of common sense or medical tests, but when it comes to finding out what your unconscious wants, muscle testing is a nice tool to try out. I learned this simple method from Julie Bermant, a psychiatric nurse practitioner who teaches people how to bring joy into times of change and transition.

To try out muscle testing, make a circle with your finger and thumb of each hand, interlinked like a chain. Say out loud: "My name is (insert your name)" while pulling the linked fingers apart using firm, steady pressure. Do it again. Now, do it again but change the name to something that is not your name: "My name is (not your name)" while pulling those fingers once more. The underlying premise is that we know, under the surface, when we are saying something that's not true. Your fingers part more easily when you are out of integrity, when you are stating something untrue for you.

I want to stress that this mode of knowing is meant to access inner, unconscious knowledge and not to replace the advice of a medical professional. It isn't scientific or objective in any way! But we aren't looking for objective insight here—we want access to your unconscious, subjective self. I use this method when I am lost in a sea of emotions—or worse—completely detaching myself from my emotions because I'm so overwhelmed.

When I was choosing whether to close my gym, I felt like I could not cry one more tear. I loved so much the daily work of running the gym, and my clients felt like family. I had developed a coaching style that lit me up from the inside and felt completely right for me. I got results for unlikely and reluctant folks by being my wacky self. But I also felt like I had completed my journey in the fitness industry, and I was tired of the lifestyle running a gym imposed. When all of my rational decision-making skills left me at a 50/50 spot, tuning into my body's wisdom helped me to uncover a reality that embarrassed me: I just didn't believe in the mission of that business anymore. I didn't want to admit it, but muscle testing let me say it out loud, first to my business partner and then to my clients as I let them know our time was coming to an end. The hard process of letting go was eased by the knowledge that I was following both my logical mind and my inner knowing.

Tool: Spontaneous Creativity

I've been making stuff since I was knee-high to a grasshopper. Brought up by parents who made everything from clothes to furniture, farmed our food, and then made stuff at work too, making came more naturally than anything else. It still does. This might not be such a fluent practice for you, but that is okay. In fact, you will probably find that the less easily creative expression comes to you the more you have to gain from tapping into it!

Which creative practice is for you? Honestly, whichever one is most easily added to your life: dancing, painting, drawing, writing poetry, sculpting, improv (or contact improv), making music. Whatever calls to you is just fine. I do suggest that you try something that is not a huge stretch financially or emotionally, so it doesn't become a burden. The goal is to give yourself a way to get in touch with yourself, not to develop mastery of a subject.

I personally find painting to be the easiest method to uncover what is kicking around inside me, especially with big canvases and big brushes and large jars of cheap paint—the bigger the better. I found that a big canvas in a medium I didn't totally understand let me immerse myself in the process. I have other creative pursuits that are about mastery; this one is always about discovery. I don't even worry about what it looks like (not easy sometimes, but worth it!). Focus on what you feel during the process and any images that come up, whether on the canvas or in your head while you do the thing. I treat these images just like dream figures: They are friendly messengers. I once wound up with an entire four-foot-square full of jellyfish. I don't know where they came from, but I know that my decision-making that weekend took quite a fluid, pulsing turn!

Tool: Divination

This is where I go from kooky-around-the-edges to full on woo. Hear me out, though. You don't need to "believe" in anything but yourself to make use of a divination tool. If you do feel the magic in your tarot deck, rock on! But if the whole idea of something called archetypal astrology or consulting a tarot deck has you running for the nearest exit, that's cool too. Consider this section entirely optional. I am generally known for my attachment to logic and reason, but over and over again I have found myself turning to divination tools when logic has abandoned me to the whims of emotional decision-making.

Each divination tool has its own language. The thing that matters is that you find ones that resonate with you and you use it respectfully. The point of a divination tool is to access what you already know inside but are struggling to put into action. Tools that might help you dive deeper into yourself include tarot, astrology, runes, scrying stones, and pendulums. The list is long. Do a little family history work and try the tools your ancient ancestors created. Using divination tools got a little strained for me when I was exposed to the impacts of colonization on traditional ways of knowing used by other cultures. I feel that the keys to making honorable use of any divination system are deep reverence and respect. Always show appropriate reverence for the tool itself and the immense efforts of those who developed them over the centuries. Actively show your respect for the tool and its origins through your actions and thoughts. I'm still learning how to interact without appropriating, and I will keep working on it.

Rituals for Closure and New Beginnings

Earlier, we explored how creating rituals builds resilience in your relationship. Rituals for reconnection and navigating sore spots are vital actions to ensuring a relationship can sustain the harsh realities of being human together. But sometimes an ending is exactly the right step. Sometimes you don't even get to choose, as an ending is thrust upon you. Ritual is essential for moving through endings without mistaking them for failures. Ritual helps us reimagine and revision relationships when you've been through hell and decide to recommit. Ritual is a way to help your soul remember that you can change, grieve, and reimagine your life even after intense loss.

Endings are new beginnings. There's your trite phrase (there would have to be one in this chapter, right?). Rather than worry about the cultural story that closing your doors or ending your relationship equals failure, I want to introduce the idea that we can learn to transition with grace and gratitude.

Common myths about endings:

- Endings are failures.

- Endings always hurt.

- We need someone else's participation to get closure.

- Persistence and longevity are more valuable than flexibility (especially when it comes to marriages!).

You are a dynamic, competent, engaged woman. You've grown a business, you've loved deeply and learned big. But you likely never got any lessons on how to use ritual to ease your transitions. Change, even positive life-affirming change, is hard. Ritual is a simple way to make it suck less. Ritual can ease this pain.

For a ritual to be maximally helpful, it should be personal and simple. You don't need anything elaborate. You don't really even need anything but yourself and a bit of time to create an effective ritual, though I have found that gathering a few meaningful items is helpful to connect fully with your intentions.

There are rituals just waiting for you to create them. My ritual templates are meant to ease the process at first, but don't hesitate to let your creativity take over! Be inventive, audacious, simple, and clear; just make it work for you today. The best ritual is one that is happening. You aren't going to feel anything new from a ritual that is constantly deferred because you're waiting for the perfect weather, setting, or people.

Bringing Closure after an Ending

Before jumping into a ritual for the ending of a relationship, I strongly suggest you do enough processing to be sure you are ready to experience the ritual deeply. The goal is to allow yourself to feel the ending and be able to move through it. Rushing the timeline while you are still numb, outraged, or swamped entirely by the emotional experience is unnecessary and not terribly effective anyways. Journal, go to therapy, splash some paint on paper, reach out to friends, listen to music, write some poetry, express yourself, watch maudlin movies, cry, and rage. Feel your feelings.

Erika wasn't sure what she needed to get over her last breakup, but she was tired of the numbness. She wanted to find her passion again because these days it was hard to be excited about anything, even though her business was going well and she knew it was a good choice to leave her boyfriend. They didn't have the same goals, she didn't like to do the same things he did, and worst of all his propensity toward misogyny had become more and more obvious as the months dragged on. Erika broke off the relationship, and she felt clear for a while but she also felt a weird sensation whenever he would text. He seemed to think that he could just keep asking and eventually she would come back. It took a ton of effort not to answer. She found herself worried that she would try to get back together with him and have to go through all of that pain again. He wasn't a good match for her, but her desire to have a boyfriend—even one who wasn't good for her—was a strong counter to her logical side. A ritual ending was just the thing to make it clear to her unconscious self that the relationship really was over, regardless of what he thought.

Action Step: Creating a Ritual for Closure

Step 1. When you are ready, gather together some physical objects to symbolically represent your relationship. For instance, a wedding ring, a picture from a shared trip, and letters from your former lover. Non-physical objects like a meaningful song or poem are equally valuable and help to bring your emotions into the mix.

Step 2. Setting aside some private time and space, open the ritual by verbally invoking protection for your heart: "I am safe. I belong in this world. My heart is protected and strong." This space and time are for you to honor and release the attachments of your relationship. Say it out loud in a way that works for you.

Step 3. Setting up the physical objects for your careful viewing, play a piece of meaningful music or read a poem that speaks the truth of your love when it was still shiny and warm.

Step 4. Allow yourself to feel.

During endings, I find it powerful to physically separate myself by cutting a braid I have made of strings or yarn that represents the ties that bound me to another. If the ending was not by my choice, this reminds me that I am making a choice to establish new, clean boundaries between myself and my former lover. The severed braid is a strong act of my will; even if I once felt this situation was happening to me, now I am making a choice for me.

I offer gratitude, verbal and genuine, for all of the parts of my life that were positively touched by this relationship and for the lessons I have learned, both wonderful and challenging. I try to get really specific here, feeling the fine details and letting myself reminisce with a gentle heart.

Close the ritual by saying goodbye and then <u>speak your boundaries</u> out loud.

"This was our relationship. I see it. I honor what it was and what it wasn't. The relationship is over, your heart is returned to you, and mine to me. The love I felt once is mine to keep."

211

Tool: Template for Creating a Ritual to Bring Closure to an Ending

Setting the space

Acknowledging emotions; be sure to include space for your grief!

Symbolic representation: Bring a physical object into the process

Acknowledging the ending with gratitude

Closing the ritual

Recommitting to Love

Sometimes things go the other way. We run into some miserable stuff, but when we do the processing and get clear about what we want we find we are actually more committed to our relationship than ever. But often this goes unmentioned and the two of you miss the chance to acknowledge the depth of experiences you have shared and make an intentional choice to move forward together. Taking the time to recommit consciously through ritual can be more enlivening than a trip to Tahiti, so don't pass it up!

Vieve and Timothy spent a lot of time working on their relationship over the past year. Before doing so, they spent months dealing with Timothy's cancer. He'd gotten through it pretty well and they were grateful for the all-clear diagnosis. But despite having gone through that all together, they felt further apart than ever. The cancer had left Timothy with some changes to his sexual functioning. He felt confused about how to connect; it kept stressing him out that sex didn't work the same as it had before. Vieve didn't mind the changes to sex, but she didn't feel the connection they had during his illness. She felt guilty and confused—who wants cancer to be part of their life? She didn't even know how to explain her feelings, so she would complain about "not being close anymore," which Timothy took as an expression of how she missed their connection through sex.

The turning point came when Vieve realized that she hadn't actually been clear about what she wanted. There was so much they still loved and enjoyed about spending their lives together, but they weren't saying any of it out loud because they were so busy <u>not saying</u> things that they were embarrassed about.

This is the perfect opportunity for using ritual to move out of the confusion by prioritizing the commitment to reconnecting. Ritual is about acknowledgement of where we are and an opportunity to set our intentions with clarity. A ritual recommitment is a chance to say to each other, "I see what we have been through and I choose us."

Once you and your partner have spent time discerning the fate of your relationship, taking the

213

time to ritualize the renewal of your commitment is a powerful step. Some people renew wedding vows for exactly this reason. There are many new starts to a loving partnership though, so don't hesitate to make a ritual just for the two of you.

Action Step: Creating a Ritual for Recommitting

Step 1. Gather something for each of you to symbolize the joy of your new commitment. It could be as simple as a stone, shell, or feather you found on a walk—no need to go down the rings route, though of course you could. I would encourage you to add a piece of music because I find that song makes it possible to revisit the mood of the moment when your commitment wobbles (and we humans do wobble from time to time!).

Step 2. Choose a space where you can feel deeply and speak to each other openly.

Step 3. Open the ritual together by lighting a candle or drawing a circle around the two of you on the ground outside. Create the sensation of a container that holds you both.

Step 4. Speak your commitment to each other. Meaning is more important than the number of words. If a poem fits the moment, that works great too!

Step 5. Share five expressions of gratitude for each other (each) by listing them verbally. Gratitude is a rock worth laying into the new foundation of your relationship.

Step 6. Exchange your physical symbolic objects.

Step 7. Eye gazing—I can't really get enough of this. I know I had you do it before, but seriously, put three to four minutes of eye gazing in. I like to start a song so no one has to look at a timer; just go until the song ends. Soft eyes, holding hands with open hearts.

Step 8. Close the ritual gently, walking out of the space together.

Tool: Template for Creating a Ritual to Recommit to a Relationship

Setting the space

Acknowledging choice and freedom to choose each other again

Symbolic representation of your intention: Ideally this is a physical object

Acknowledging the change and commitment ahead with gratitude

Closing the ritual

Key Takeaways

- Change is inevitable in all of life: relationships, business, the whole shebang.

- Endings do not equal failures. Did you learn something? Then I'd say it isn't a failure.

- Deciding whether to continue or call time on a relationship can feel overwhelming. This is a time you might want to turn to intuitive tools to crack open any blocks you are feeling.

- This culture puts a lot of emphasis on the longevity of relationships but there are plenty of other ways to measure the success of your love, like how gracefully you can transition from lovers to friends, how much you taught each other, what you created together, or how much you learned from the experience.

- Rituals that mark the endings and recommitments in our relationships deepen the meaning they carry and make it easier to integrate the lessons learned.

Chapter 13

Conclusion and Celebrations!

Congratulations, you've now undertaken a more thorough relationship education than most people get in a lifetime! You exposed yourself to new ways of knowing yourself and your strengths. You learned how to apply your entrepreneurial spirit to find deep intimacy with your partner. You faced the challenges of creating your loving relationships intentionally, with explicit language and loving rituals of reconnection. You deepened your knowledge of self by looking in the mirror of Otherness. You learned new ways to approach the toughest parts of day-to-day life with respect for each other, and you've got a few tricks up your sleeve for getting your partner and yourself on the same team when life is overwhelming.

Assessment: Your Project Relationship Wins

You've undertaken a process of intense self-reflection and relational reflection throughout this book. I'm excited because I've seen how this work transforms lives. It can be easy to miss in your own life though, taking for granted where you are today and neglecting to see how far you've come. It is a big deal! You are a rock star for taking on the challenge!

Take a few minutes to check in with your body and soul and see where you are right now. Three deep breaths, slow and easeful, then reflect on where you are today.

- Three words that describe your business today:

- Three words that describe how you are showing up in your business right now:

- Three words that describe your relationship today:

- Three words that describe how you show up in the relationship:

- Three words that describe how your partner shows up (from your view) in the relationship:

You first assessed these aspects of your life in Chapter 2. Take a few minutes to notice the changes. What areas have shifted? Was it easy? Where did you notice resistance?

You've been engaged in actively creating your life. It isn't always pretty. You may have faced some inner demons and processed some painful memories. Hopefully this work feels mostly playful, but I know that the Project Relationship action steps may have led you into the darker territory of your soul. The trick to getting the absolute most out of self-awareness work is to keep at it. That can feel hard when the work is sometimes dark.

To make your inner work a sustainable practice, you need just one more move: celebration!

Celebrate the ability to say sexy words out loud! Celebrate having named some of your complexes! Celebrate taking a few minutes to practice kissing! Celebrate having that tough conversation about emotional labor! Celebrate your experience of growth!

Celebrations don't need to be limited to the prosaic dinner out (though I will literally never turn down dinner at my favorite restaurant). We can bring joyful, celebratory vibes to any moment with as little as a smile and a high five. Make every day an excuse to celebrate by turning toward love: love of yourself, love of your partner, love of the freaking amazing weirdness of being a human. Turn up the celebratory energy by laughing together. Watch some comedy or, better yet, make some by playing together! Whatever brings you joy, go for it.

Thank you for coming along on this messy, wonder-filled adventure of the soul with me. I'm honored to have had a place in your experience for a while. If you would like to stay in touch, please join me at www.JoliHamilton.com for free worksheet downloads, new adventures, and the opportunity to connect to other folks creating their best life through self-awareness.

Bonus Chapter 14

Treasure Hunting in the Wilds of Your Soul

You've just spent significant time and energy learning how to leverage your entrepreneurial skills to create the relationship you were always meant to have. Relating isn't the kind of thing you can do and then check off a list, though. You'll constantly find new situations drag old problems to the surface. Luckily, this isn't the total bummer it seems because these "same old problems" can help us learn who we are in a way nothing else can. This chapter is filled with three of the juiciest opportunities for inner knowing I've ever found. Some of them we've touched on already; this is a deeper dive into the benefits of applied depth psychology.

Recurring challenges feel terrible. You do the work, make some progress, and then out of nowhere you find yourself right back in the same old mess. When a problem comes up over and over again without seeming to change, even if we spend time trying to change, it's quite likely you've become aware of a psychological complex. This sticky spot in your unconscious is demanding your attention, usually in a way that causes trouble for you. Over a hundred years ago, depth psychologist C. G. Jung defined complex as a set of emotions, memories, and perceptions centered on a common theme. Everyone has complexes. They are completely normal, but they often get a bit out of hand. At that point, the person <u>caught in the grip</u> of the complex has irrational feelings and thoughts about a particular aspect of life to a degree that upsets their ability to self-regulate or maintain a feeling of psychological balance. Jung put it simply when he said that everyone knows they have complexes, but they often can't see when the complex <u>has them</u>. But that's how complexes work; they trip us up and are a natural part of us. Sigh.

I put the notion of the complex to use in my life by imagining how my early memories and the most painful experiences of my life left a little Velcro spot on my soul—a place where it is easy for more psychological energy to get caught even years later. It is tempting to blame our parents or other caregivers for these complexes. Certainly, I wish that traumatic events never happened to anyone. But I don't find it especially useful to worry about that. Having raised seven children myself, I know that I have left the fingerprints of my pain upon them despite my valiant efforts not to do so. Regardless of how gentle our childhoods might have been, we will have complexes of some sort.

A piece of Jung's complex theory often overlooked by modern readers is his assertion that without complexes, we would be psychologically dead. Those sticky spots provide somewhere for our life experiences to collect and organize. I picture them a bit like tide pools by the ocean. If you look into a single tide pool, you'll see ocean water teeming with interesting life. Some of it seems to be suffering in the enclosed space, some of it thriving. Look at the next tide pool down the beach and you'll find an entirely different but similarly exciting mix of life and energy doing exactly what life does—living, being, becoming, dying. Complex theory helps me remember the paradox of trauma: I am far more than the traumatic events that happened to me, but those things do matter. I can take it one moment at a time while I learn to integrate and individuate. This is an ongoing process, not an event.

Projection

Noticing complexes begins internally. Don't try to look at your partner or friends and label their complexes. First, it's just not going to help them; they need to do their own self-awareness work. Second, it is easy to see our own complexes "out there" in other people. Humans are funny: We see ourselves best not in a glass mirror but in the mirror of another person. The image will be distorted (hey, it is being passed through two psyches and all), but what we see when we look at others can tell us loads about ourselves. The trouble is that we usually mistake what we see as something that belongs entirely to the other person. In other words, when we are projecting bits of our best and worst qualities out onto others, we tend to forget that we are the ones doing the projecting. It's not that they don't carry the quality we see, it's just that we should probably look at how that quality shows up in us before we start making judgements and telling others what to do with themselves.

Complexes are slippery things, though. They can masquerade as bad habits or pet peeves, escaping our notice. But a complex is worth bringing to consciousness because it has a bigger and more far-reaching effect than we realize. Because a complex is rooted in the unconscious, this isn't going to be the easiest work you ever do. But doing it means the difference between growing up and owning your own shit, and remaining in immature, self-limiting patterns your whole life.

Shadow

Jung said that the first complex each of us must come to grips with is the shadow. Later, Robert Bly described the shadow as a long bag slung over our shoulder, into which we deposit all the qualities that our parents don't like, the parts of us that teachers need to weed out, the personality nuances despised by our peers and lovers. When we are growing up, we continually put more and more of ourselves into the long bag, dragging it behind us as we try to fit into one mold after another. Of course, humans are social critters. We adapt to the preferences and rules of our society as best we can. We seek our place in the social world by putting away the bits of us that are pointed out as disruptive, problematic, or wrong. The problem is that those asking us to refine ourselves are not objective truth-tellers. They are flawed, wounded people themselves. Our social constructs are not inviolable rules without bias. And so we cut away pieces of ourselves in an almost random pattern, owing to the unique environment in which we live. We take the individual we were and stow away some of our most challenging, and some of our best, qualities. The long bag grows. The shadow contains more and more of who we are.

Figuring out that I had a father complex made dealing with my partner a completely different story. Yep, that's right, I have daddy issues. I'm not ashamed about it. It's just how my life happened to unfold. My dad didn't do anything horrible, he just didn't know how to really see me and participate in my childhood in a way that I needed. I was too young to ask for what I needed. Buried in my unconscious is the imprint left by a lack of empathic mirroring. In other words, when I least expect it, I will act *as if* my (very masculine) partner is repeating the patterns of my childhood. See the emphasis there? I place myself at the center of the action. It's far less relevant to question the objective reality of the situation. When we are caught up by a complex, the subjective meaning of how we feel the experience is what really counts.

Naming our psychological complexes is a great way to start noticing where you get caught over and over again by particular things. Money, our parents, sex, body image are all common complexes. It would be far more unusual to not have a complex around one of these topics than for you to have some inner work to do around them. Getting to know your complexes is a great way to get to know your true self better. By naming the complexes that come up over and over again, you can claim the constructive, positive, helpful stuff confidently. And though it isn't terribly fun, you can also work with the destructive aspects of your complexes and start to ease yourself out of feeling possessed by something beyond your control.

I am very grateful for the influence depth psychological training has had on my life, but I don't confine my ideas to the strict classical Jungian ways. Instead, I take Jung at his word when he said the best we could do for our collective psychological well-being is to dream the dream forward and not get stuck being pedantic about what he (or anyone) wrote about the psyche. I use Jung's complex theory in whatever way proves useful for myself, my kids, and my clients.

Complexes become much more tenable once you name them. You don't have to limit yourself to some prescribed list of complexes. I shared having a father complex earlier because it's one most people have heard mentioned, at least in bad jokes. Remember, a complex is just stuck energy—a pattern that plays out with annoying regularity.

Action Step: A Beginner's Guide to Dancing with Your Complexes

Step 1. Notice. Where are you repeating an argument? What can you not seem to move past? When do you find yourself thinking *what the hell am I doing, this isn't like me!*

Step 2. Name it. This is personal. The complex has an archetypal core, which means that it has a sort of universal basis, but the way it comes to life in you is totally individual. Perhaps you have some of the common complexes at work: money, body image, or those old chestnuts, the mother and father complexes. I certainly do. But you can name the complexes whatever works for you. The trick to naming a complex is to keep in mind that your complex is yours. It has very little to do with the present situation with your father, for instance. He might still be tripping you up when you go visit for the holidays, but the present-day father-daughter experience isn't where the complex gets its energy. The complex is dug way down in the depths of your soul. Your relationship to everything fatherly in the universe is tied to this complex. Sounds huge, right? It is.

I hope you're still with me. I am an action-first, results-oriented kinda woman myself. But complex theory is worth the time, I promise. Armed with information about complexes, you can have an entirely new understanding of the parts of yourself and your partner, especially the stuff that has most mystified you up till now.

Repeat this process a few times, but don't try to pin down all your complexes. You can't—none of us can—and it would be a waste of time to try. The ones that need naming right now are tied to the issues that are tripping you up right now. Look at where you are constantly suffering—that area needs work. Maybe it is in a professional area, maybe it's personal. Often, the same complex is activated across all areas of your life; it just looks different in each arena. For instance, a father complex might look like a profound desire for control in business and at home. It might be that at home you act out a defensive, angry resistance toward any authority on the part of your partner, while at work it just looks like being a skillful leader. It takes time to sort this all out. You don't have to do it all at once. Just notice and name for now.

Gathering All the Pieces of Yourself

So, there are your complexes, kicking your butt under the surface, making you feel a little off-balance and funky. What does this have to do with having awesome relationships? Everything. Because our complexes lurk around in our unconscious, they pop up to the surface by getting projected all over other people, especially those we love very much.

The terms *projection* and *projective identification* make the process I'm about to offer you sound a bit stuffy, and

228

it is a concept more than a century old, rooted in the early days when some old white men were creating the field of psychology and trying very hard to make it all very scientific, even mechanical if they could. But freeing yourself from projections is more an art than a science in my experience. Reclaiming and recollecting the pieces of yourself that someone else found icky or difficult is a creative act. Why creative? Because in order to reclaim the bits of yourself projected all over the place, you have to tap into your imagination. You have to let yourself see past the easy, obvious reasons why someone drives you mad and imagine how that stuff is a part of you. You have to notice how you see wondrous things in other people but can't own those qualities in yourself. When you start to work with your projections, you will be recreating your self-concept. It is big, beautiful, creative work.

Working with projection is a practice rather than an event because there is nothing unnatural about projecting. It's just part of how it is to be human. It's impractical to hope that you'll transcend all projection. You aren't going to stop projecting; you are just going to spend a bit of energy paying attention to what and where you are projecting (and what's getting projected all over you).

So, how does projection work? Think of how you would style your hair—you could do it anywhere but usually you stand in front of a mirror because it is so much easier to see what you are doing that way.

Projecting some of your stuff out onto other people is a lot like that—except if we do it unconsciously we are using a person as if they were an object. Big red flag! You don't want to do that, but our unconscious is crafty. If we don't feel comfortable and confident about something, the unconscious has no problem "seeing" that quality out in the world rather than in us. You know that phrase, "whatever drives you bonkers about someone else is really annoying you about yourself"? Yeah, that's just another way of saying look in the mirror and pull back that projection. Let's say that you really struggle with your mother-in-law. Maybe you feel she is really controlling, sticking her nose into your marriage and overstepping boundaries. You feel like she never shows anyone else respect. Instead, she thinks her decisions are the best and she should be involved with everything in her grown son's life. At first, it wasn't so bad. You thought she was attentive, but these days you feel frustrated at her every move. Now, the thing is, your mother-in-law can absolutely BE a person with control issues AND this might still be a projection on your part.

Huh?

Yeah, the annoying thing about projections is that they need something to "stick" to. They're like those little burrs that stick onto a fuzzy sock when you are out hiking but will probably not cover your denim jeans. Your mother-in-law is a useful person for your projection; she has enough controlling habits to give you a place to stick your fears and distaste for your own controlling tendencies. That way, you can see that frustrating behavior out there safely separate from you. You can both observe and disown your controlling self. Cool.

Except by projecting "control" onto her and complaining to your best friend, partner, and kids about how maddening she is, you are not working on the thing you can actually change in your life. You know what I'm going to say. It's annoying and true. The only place you can make change is within yourself. You can ask for change in others, but you can't make them change.

So, what can you do? You can start looking for your projections. It's usually easiest to spot one like I have just described. Someone close who makes you feel frustrated, annoyed, or tired, just by being themselves. I'm not talking about someone who is abusing their power, manipulating your life to suit their needs (that's another level of problem), but someone who is a decent person but who ticks you off with tiny things.

I'm suggesting this kind of projection because there are always small frustrations in our life. If we were to cut out every single person who irritated us, we would get pretty lonely. Attending to our projections is self-empowering because it puts the action back on your side of the relationship. You can stop worrying about what your mother-in-law is doing and tend to your soul, your experience of life. There may indeed be boundaries that must be set in order to restore respect to your relationship, but starting to recall your projections will free up your energy to focus on creating the life you want, beginning with your relationships.

Your Golden Shadow

It's common to assume that the projections we make are negative, difficult-to-own qualities. There is another kind of shadow though, one often referred to as a golden shadow, and this is the one I want you to take a look at first. The golden shadow is a quality we personally revere, we wish we had, we think would LOVE to claim, but for some reason cannot bear to recognize in ourselves. These are qualities like intelligence, practicality, gentleness, or boldness. I know, this sounds silly. Why would you pretend not to be something you value? Why would you struggle to see some of your own best qualities? Remember that long bag we talked about where you stuffed all the things you learned not to be? Yup, a bunch of that stuff is freaking fantastic. Along the way while you were growing up, you were convinced to cut off some of your you-ness. Even the absolute best caregiver doesn't see us perfectly. They have their own baggage. It's okay, no need to blame anyone. Let's just deal with it! Time to figure out where we are projecting our awesomeness and reclaim it!

In case you struggle with the idea of putting yourself first, let me help you out of that hole. While a golden shadow doesn't feel quite as damning as a negative shadow quality for the person we project it upon, it is still an unhelpful burden. Either way, we are unconsciously asking another to carry a piece of our psyche. The golden shadow needs to be reclaimed—for you both!

Action Step: Seeing Your Golden Shadow

Part 1. The feeling we call falling in love is a wonderful clue to the golden shadow. Recall the very first exercise where you mined your memory for the sparks that first occurred between you and your love. Dig back into that memory.

What did you admire about them most? Pay special attention to those things that seemed really luminous about them. Keep it short, one or two words to describe each aspect (examples: grace, intelligence, boldness).

Pick one to work with first. Where does this quality show up in you? It is important not to compare yourself to your partner—this isn't about who has more of the quality. Just ask yourself whether it lives in you as well. Perhaps it takes a different form or shows up in a different area of life. Was this a quality you longed for when you were younger or something you wished others had recognized in you?

If you don't see it in yourself at all, dig a bit deeper with this bonus step:

Ask a friend if they can see these qualities in you. It can be really hard to own some of our really awesome qualities, so let someone else hold up a mirror for you.

Part 2. I encourage you to repeat this exercise looking for where your golden shadow has been projected onto someone in your professional life. Who do you admire? Who in your field strikes you almost mute with awe? Take a long look. What are you projecting onto them that you find difficult to claim in yourself?

Reclaiming and Recollecting the Darker Stuff

After you've started to recognize your golden shadow projections, hopefully you'll feel ready to dig a bit deeper. It's time to look at some of the less palatable stuff you've projected and had projected onto you. I've tried pulling this exercise apart into separate pieces but honestly, the mess that projection causes is easier to look at without trying to make it neat and tidy like some kind of emotional algebra problem. When it comes to the people we have our most intimate relationships with—our lovers, parents, kids, and chosen family—the web of interconnected projections is too complicated for tidiness. Life and love are messy. Let's just be with the mess.

That said, this is tender work. Evaluate your current situation. Do you have enough bandwidth to explore this right now? Do you have self-care practices in place that will support you as you take on a deep look in the mirror? If not, I would actually suggest tabling this exercise for a better time. That is not easy for me to say because this is really valuable work and I know you will benefit from taking it on, but it is super important that you be able to manage the emotions that come along with it. This exercise looks fairly short, but you can mine these questions over and over again. I've used this particular exercise on myself at least once a year for five years and I always turn up something new.

Action Step: Recollecting Projections

This is another opportunity to look at both your professional and personal worlds. We usually have many projections going on simultaneously, just running along under the surface of things.

Repeat this exercise for your lover, your work life, and even your extended family or community. This is a crucial step in claiming your autonomy—in learning to live your life—not the one people attempt to manipulate you into (well-meaning or not, manipulation through projection is so common!).

- What am I projecting onto someone else?

- What qualities can I not stand in someone else? What drives me nuts in my partner, in a pet peeve sort of way?

- Where is this quality in me?

- Have I disowned a part of myself and projected it onto my partner?

- What is someone else projecting onto me?

- Have I been in a situation where I thought "that's not like me" or caught myself acting completely unfamiliarly? Have I been placed into a role or position in someone else's life that I did not consent to? Have I been the object of someone's obsession?

Each of the ideas in this bonus chapter can be life changing, and they aren't a one-shot deal. Come back to these ideas whenever life is spinning around you or you feel tempted to play the blame game in your relationship. Just as we talked about in the beginning, give yourself a chance to honestly evaluate yourself and you'll be on your way to reimagining your relationship and what you want from it from a place of deep intimacy.

Acknowledgements

Every client, student, or customer I ever had taught me something about being the best version of myself. Without their presence, I wouldn't have been an entrepreneur at all—many of my businesses began because someone asked me to start. To the parents who welcomed me into the birthing process as their doula, to the brides who trusted me to design a gown they would sparkle in, to the sweaty gaggle of athletes who kept me laughing during the darkest days of my life, to the women who trust me to help them craft a life that finally feels like home, and so many others in so many other ways, thank you. I am an entrepreneur because you connected with me and let me be part of your life. Each of you has a place in my heart.

This book would not have come into being without the inspiration and encouragement of Angela Lussier. When I couldn't see the (um...super obvious) themes running through my life, she asked exactly the questions I needed to answer.

My team at Paper Raven Books made the publishing process that seemed so overwhelming into a manageable thing to add to my ridiculously complicated life.

My kids, Sage, Rhys, Moia, Torin, Logan, Quinn, and MacEwan somehow managed to live through my writing a dissertation and this book at the same time. Thank you for cooking dinners when I was too tired, washing <u>all</u> the dishes, and most of all for being a wild bunch of adventurers in the unknown. Parenting you is the hardest and easiest stuff I've ever done. Thanks for bearing with me as I grow and change too.

And of course, Ken, my dragon, who surprised me with his very existence and who is always excited when I want to have the tough conversations, explore the darkness within, or need someone to listen to the millions of new ideas I have. Without our relationship— the good, the horrible, and the boring bits—I would not have believed that deep, fiery passion and healing, peaceful harmony could coexist in one marriage. Thank you for treating my dreams with the same care you treat your own and for being more interested in growth than comfort.

Notes

Chapter 1: Getting By, Wanting More

Badal, S. B. (2020, April 08). *What Drives Entrepreneurial Success?* Retrieved from https://news.gallup.com/businessjournal/184895/drives-entrepreneurial-success.aspx

Kerr, S. P., Kerr, W., & Xu, T. (2017). Personality Traits of Entrepreneurs: A Review of Recent Literature. *National Bureau of Economic Research.* Working Paper 24097. doi:10.3386/w24097

López-Núñez, M., Rubio-Valdehita, S., Aparicio-García, M., & Díaz-Ramiro, E. (2020). Are Entrepreneurs Born or Made? The Influence of Personality. *Personality and Individual Differences, 154.* doi:10.1016/j.paid.2019.109699

McDonald, T. M., Marshall, M. I., & Delgado, M. S. (2017). Is Working with Your Spouse Good for Business? The Effect of Working with Your Spouse on Profit for Rural Businesses. *Journal of Family and Economic Issues, 38*(4), 477–493. doi:10.1007/s10834-017-9525-8

Owens, G., Scott, J. M., & Blenkinsopp, J. (2013). The Impact of Spousal Relationships on Business Venture Success. Institute for Small Business & Entrepreneurship conference. Cardiff, UK.

Chapter 2: Empowered Relating

Luca, M. R., & Robu, A. (2016). Personality Traits in Entrepreneurs and Self-Employed. *Bulletin of the Transylvania University of Brasov, 9*(2), 92–98. Retrieved August 4, 2020.

Chapter 3: Boundaries, the Invitation to Intimacy

Clifton, J., & Bharadwaj Badal, S. (2014). *Entrepreneurial Strengthsfinder*. New York, NY: Gallup Press.

Chapter 4: Who Is This Person?

Chapman, G. (2019, March 13). Discover Your Love Language. Retrieved from https://www.5lovelanguages.com/

Perel, E. (2006). *Mating in Captivity: Reconciling the Erotic and the Domestic*. New York, NY: HarperCollins.

Chapter 5: Relationship Resilience

de Botton, A. (2018). *The Course of Love*. Toronto: Signal.

Chapter 6: Courageous Connecting

Jones, D. (2015, January 09). *The 36 Questions That Lead to Love*. Retrieved from https://www.nytimes.com/2015/01/11/style/36-questions-that-lead-to-love.html

Chapter 7: Getting What You Need

Guggenbühl-Craig, A. (2008). *Marriage Is Dead - Long Live Marriage!* Putnam, CT: Spring Publications.

Chapter 8: Sex

Harris, S. (2018). *Tongue Tied: Untangling Communication in Sex, Kink, and Relationships*. Jersey City, NJ: Cleis Press.

Try New Things. (n.d.). Retrieved from http://www.mojoupgrade.com/

Chapter 9: Fighting with Love

Danes, S. M., & Morgan, E. A. (2004). Family Business-Owning Couples: An EFT View into Their Unique Conflict Culture. *Contemporary Family Therapy, 26*(3), 241–260. doi:10.1023/b:coft.0000037913.20921.0e

Gottman, J., & Gottman, J. S. (2018). *The Science of Couples and Family Therapy: Behind the Scenes at the Love Lab*. New York, NY: W.W Norton & Company.

Chapter 10: Talking Business with Love

Sex and Relationship Coach: Marie-Claire Thauvette. (2020, June 18). Retrieved from https://relationshipbliss.ca/

Chapter 11: Talking Money with Love

Dew, J., Britt, S., & Huston, S. (2012). Examining the Relationship Between Financial Issues and Divorce. *Family Relations, 61*(4), 615–628. doi:10.1111/j.1741-3729.2012.00715.x

Chapter 12: When Things Fall Apart

Pinkola Estes, C. (2003). *A Beginner's Guide to Dream Interpretation: Uncover the Hidden Riches of Your Dreams with Jungian Analyst Clarissa Pinkola Estes.* Louisville, CO: Sounds True.

Bonus Chapter 14: Treasure Hunting in the Wilds of Your Soul

Bly, R. C., & Booth, W. C. (1988). *A Little Book on the Human Shadow.* San Francisco, CA: Harper & Row.

Jung, C. G. (1959/1990). *The Collected Works of C. G. Jung, Vol. 9, Part 1. Archetypes and the Collective Unconscious.* (R. F. C. Hull, Trans.). Princeton, NJ: Princeton University Press.

Jung, C. G. (1971/1990). *The Collected Works of C. G. Jung, Vol.6. Psychological Types.* (R. F. C. Hull, Trans.). Princeton, NJ: Princeton University Press.

CPSIA information can be obtained
at www.ICGtesting.com
Printed in the USA
LVHW060714011120
670162LV00011B/68